WHEN YOUR ADULT CHILD STRAYS

ALSO BY JIM BURNS

Confident Parenting

Creating an Intimate Marriage

10 Building Blocks for a Solid Family

Closer (with Cathy Burns)

Understanding Your Teen

Pass It On

The Purity Code

Teaching Your Children Healthy Sexuality

God Made Your Body (children's book)

How God Makes Babies (children's book)

Getting Ready for Marriage (with Doug Fields)

The First Few Years of Marriage (with Doug Fields)

Faith Conversations for Families

Doing Life with Your Adult Children

Have Serious Fun

Finding Joy in the Empty Nest

WHEN YOUR ADULT CHILD STRAYS

TRADING HEARTACHE FOR HOPE

JIM BURNS

ZONDERVAN BOOKS

When Your Adult Child Strays

Published by Zondervan, 3950 Sparks Drive SE, Suite 101, Grand Rapids, MI 49546, USA. Zondervan is a registered trademark of The Zondervan Corporation, L.L.C., a wholly owned subsidiary of HarperCollins Christian Publishing, Inc.

Requests for information should be addressed to customercare@harpercollins.com.

Zondervan titles may be purchased in bulk for educational, business, fundraising, or sales promotional use. For information, please email SpecialMarkets@Zondervan.com.

ISBN 978-0-310-37047-5 (softcover)
ISBN 978-0-310-37052-9 (audio)
ISBN 978-0-310-37049-9 (ebook)

Published in association with the literary agency of WordServe Literary Group, Ltd., www.wordserveliterary.com.

HarperCollins Publishers, Macken House, 39/40 Mayor Street Upper, Dublin 1, D01 C9W8, Ireland (https://www.harpercollins.com)

Cover design: James W. Hall IV
Cover illustration: Klaus Vedfelt / Getty Images
Interior design: Denise Froehlich

To Cindy Ward

Thank you for your more than twenty years of partnering in the work at HomeWord. Our entire family adores you. Cathy and I are so grateful for all the extra effort you put into making HomeWord such a special place to work and serve. We respect and admire you. We are deeply grateful. Thank you for all you do for so many.

CONTENTS

PREFACE

When I wrote *Doing Life with Your Adult Children: Keep Your Mouth Shut and the Welcome Mat Out*,[1] I never imagined that it would open the door to years of hearing deeply personal stories from parents carrying heartbreak, disappointment, grief, shame, confusion, anger, and guilt—sometimes interwoven with moments of joy. I could easily add twenty-five more words to the list of things a parent feels when their adult child strays and violates their values.

Behind nearly every adult child who has strayed from their family's values, there is a parent carrying deep pain. From the moment your child is born, their life becomes entwined with yours—and that bond doesn't weaken with time. Many parents have told me that their adult children's struggles have consumed their thoughts, their energy, even their sense of peace. Few parents are truly prepared for the heartache that comes when a grown child fails to thrive, makes destructive choices, falters, or seems lost in life. Most of the time, adult children's behaviors and poor choices are not about a parent. But that doesn't keep us from blaming ourselves:

- "It was because of the divorce."
- "We were too strict."

1. Jim Burns, *Doing Life with Your Adult Children: Keep Your Mouth Shut and the Welcome Mat Out* (Zondervan, 2019).

- "I was too lenient."
- "I worked outside the home."
- "As a single parent, I was just too distracted."
- "Our marriage was so bad that we were a poor example."
- "We should have prayed more."
- "I shouldn't have kicked my son out of the house."
- "I should have kicked my son out of the house."

And the list goes on, but you get the picture and probably have your own story of blame to tell.

This is a book of hope. While we'll be diving into the messy, complex, and sometimes painful realities of navigating life with adult children, we won't shy away from the hard truths. Some of the challenges are deep and difficult, and solutions aren't always simple or a quick fix. After all, we are all human. We all miss the mark, and even the most successful families are far from perfect. Most of us can relate to this line from the Disney movie *Lilo and Stitch*: "This is my family. . . . It's little, and broken, but still good. Yeah. Still good."[2]

I firmly believe, however, that even in the middle of painful and uncertain circumstances, we can discover a healthier, more peaceful place for our families. While we always hope for change, sometimes the situation doesn't improve the way we imagined. Walking with an adult child who has strayed isn't a quick fix. It's a marathon, not a sprint. It requires patience,

---

2. *Lilo and Stitch*, written and directed by Chris Sanders and Dean De Blois (Walt Disney Feature Animation, 2002).

resilience, and the willingness to stay engaged for the long haul. My hope and prayer is that the principles shared in this book will not only encourage and inspire you but also bring healing to some of the brokenness you may experience along the way. But know that *easy* doesn't appear anywhere on these pages.

One of my best friends in life, a man who is closer than a brother, has an adult daughter who took a drastic detour from the values she was raised with. He and his wife are two of the finest people and parents I know. They are consistent, loving, caring, filled with integrity, and an inspiration to the rest of us. Nevertheless, Amber Joy[3] gave them a run for their money. Their story is still being written.

Amber is beautiful and brilliant. Fun and adventuresome. She also had some tough things happen to her at a young age that her parents didn't know about. Amber fell into a life of promiscuity, alcohol, and drugs. She wasn't a bad kid, but the drugs she was using to medicate her pain pulled her strongly in a direction that caused her to violate their family values and stray from their deep-rooted faith.

There were nights when Amber's parents had no idea where she was and times when they feared for her life. Her young adult years were marked by one treatment program after another—thousands of dollars spent, each effort followed by another heartbreaking setback. Still, her parents pressed on. They chose to stand by her, offering love and

3. In almost all cases, names have been changed to protect confidentiality.

support while also applying many of the boundaries and principles shared in this book. Eventually she turned a corner. She has now been clean and sober for five years, with a few bumps along the way.

This journey is far from over—it will continue, with its share of highs and lows—but my dear friends chose to stay in it. They did the hard work. They built a support system around themselves. And today their relationship with their daughter is grounded in love, trust, and genuine connection.

Recently they gave their daughter a necklace that had three words inscribed: Peace-Joy-Hope. They told her their prayer was that she would have peace with her past, joy today, and hope for tomorrow.

That's my prayer for you as you read this book.

THE NINE PRINCIPLES TO *DOING LIFE WITH YOUR ADULT CHILDREN*

PRINCIPLE 1:

You're fired! Your role as the parent must change.

PRINCIPLE 2:

Keep your mouth shut and the welcome mat out: Unsolicited advice is usually taken as criticism.

PRINCIPLE 3:

Why is it taking my kid so long to grow up? You can't ignore your child's culture.

PRINCIPLE 4:

How to raise an entitled adult child . . . or not: They will never know how far the town is if you carry them on your back.

PRINCIPLE 5:

A failure to launch: Your job is to move them from dependence to independence.

PRINCIPLE 6:

When your grown child violates your values: You can't want it more than they want it.

PRINCIPLE 7:

The high cost of money: Financial independence and responsibility is the goal.

PRINCIPLE 8:

In-laws, stepfamilies, and the blend: Wear beige and keep your mouth shut.

PRINCIPLE 9:

It's party time with the grandkids: Being a grandparent may be your greatest legacy.[1]

---

1. Jim Burns, *Doing Life with Your Adult Children: Keep Your Mouth Shut and the Welcome Mat Out* (Zondervan, 2019).

CHAPTER 1

FROM HEARTACHE TO HOPE

Few heartaches cut as deeply as watching an adult child drift away from the values and faith that once bound you together. You pray. You hope. You question. You pray again, and sometimes it doesn't get better; it gets more complicated. You begin to feel unsettled in every way, right down to your heart. Watching the child you once rocked to sleep, sang lullabies to, celebrated first steps with, and spent countless hours cheering at soccer games or dance recitals walk away from the hopes and dreams you had for their life can be deeply heartbreaking. You stood by them through the awkward teenage years—navigating school struggles, relationship ups and downs, and all the growing pains—still feeling somewhat in control. But then one day, you look up and ask yourself, "What happened to that child I knew so well?" You quickly realize they don't know how to be an adult, and you don't know how to be the parent of an adult. You know it has something to do with reinventing your relationship and relinquishing control. You've invested the last two decades guiding, nurturing, and making decisions—and now, suddenly, you're no longer in control. You are miles away from their childhood, and it sometimes feels like they are miles away from your values.

If your heart is broken because of your adult child's choices, you're not alone; you've joined countless parents around the world who are walking through the same painful emotions. Far too often parents suffer in silent shame, when the best thing they can do is lean into hope. But you can seldom do that in isolation.

I recently received a text from a friend telling me about her two "prodigal adult children." She opened her text with these words, "It's been quite a journey." People would be amazed by how often I see a note or hear a question that begins with that phrase. But maintaining a relationship with our adult children really is a journey. Depending on our health, we will be in relationship with adult children longer than those two decades we raised them and launched them to adulthood.

Here is the best advice I can give you: "Stay in the journey." Persevere. Don't quit. Stick with it for the long haul. Remember that you're not alone. Sometimes the journey gets weary. It brings joy sometimes and deep sorrow at others, but no matter what, do whatever it takes to endure. Don't let heartbreak drive you to despair. Here's a heartache-to-hope story to encourage you.

Meet Eric

Not only was Eric raised in a loving Christian home, but his parents were also in ministry in a thriving, healthy church. His dad was a dynamic leader and an engaged father. Eric's mom was the nurturing center of the home. They would be the first to say their home was far from perfect, but it wasn't crazy either. Eric had not been an easy child to raise, but his parents were caught by surprise when he went away to college and then left their values and faith. Eric spent two years in college experimenting with drugs, alcohol, and sexual promiscuity. Not unlike some pastors' kids who leave home, he rebelled and yet showed respect for his parents when he was home. He simply had a penchant for partying and was enticed by a secular lifestyle.

Eric's story was more of a steady drift than an all-out rebellion. He dropped out of college, traveled, played in a band, and hopped from job to job. He was involved in several short-term romantic relationships. He was definitely the "noncommitment" type of guy. The time between visits to see his family got farther and farther apart. He finally settled down and married a girl who was unquestionably not in his family "circle of trust." Fortunately, they didn't have children before the marriage fell apart.

Eric's mom told me that one of the hardest days of her life was when she took her wayward son out to lunch and he emphatically proclaimed that he was an atheist and wanted nothing to do with his parents' faith. He said, "At least I'm not living a hoax like my other brother and sister." He added, "You and Dad were good parents, but you just don't get real life. I'm going to do what I want to do, and it doesn't include God or faith or your morals." Even though this event had taken place years earlier, Eric's mom's eyes teared up when she told me the story.

After Eric had wandered for fifteen years with hundreds of stops and starts in life, his parents were losing hope that he would ever come back "home." Eric was carrying the weight of his choices, and his parents were genuinely sad. Then one day in year fifteen in the middle of a Sunday morning church service, Eric slipped into the seat beside his mother and reached for her hand. She said tears streamed down her face throughout the rest of the service while Eric kept hold of her hand. He smiled and whispered, "Mom, this is a bit much." She told me she didn't stop crying for most of three days. Eric was back. He was home. The prodigal had returned, and she traded her heartache for a sincere hope. This may not be your story, but there is much we can learn from it that is key to our own life situations with our adult children who stray. Following are a few takeaways.

Stay in the Story

Eric's parents stayed in the story. They realized they were playing the long game. Playing the long game means taking the necessary steps to set yourself up for long-term success. That same principle applies to finances, staying in shape, developing a good marriage, and dealing with our adult children. Even in tough times, staying in the relationship for the long haul and being present in adult kids' lives is most often the answer. When parents of adult children come to me for advice, they're sometimes unsettled by what I tell them—because it often involves discipline, perseverance, grit, and the courage to remain present in the messy middle of the relationship. Pain is part of life. We face either the pain of discipline or the pain of regret. I encourage parents to choose the pain that comes with staying engaged—to be willing to hold back from saying everything they think, and to give their adult children the space to grow through their own experiences. This may sound overwhelming, but there's freedom in letting go of control and simply showing up with love. I know, it's not easy.

Part of staying in the story comes back to living with grit, determination, and patience. Playing the long game means paying a small price today to make tomorrow's improved relationship with your adult child flourish. Author, speaker, and researcher Angela Duckworth's TED Talk on grit is one of the most widely viewed, and she later expanded it into a bestselling book.[1] She studied successful people in business and education and found it wasn't the most talented or smartest people who succeeded over the years. It was the people with grit. I think the same is true with parents of adult children. Grit in a relationship has to do with courage, resolve, and strength of character on your part. Grit is bravery, backbone, determination, patience, strength of will, and resolve. Don't those things sound like a lot of fun? No, grit is your passion for a better relationship with your adult child combined with perseverance to stay in that relationship even if the child is breaking your heart. Developing grit in the relationship says, "I will do whatever it takes. If it's counseling, I'll go to counseling. If it means saying I'm sorry, I'll do it. If it means putting time and attention into improving the relationship, I'm in."

Here is how Angela Duckworth expresses it: "Grit is

1. Angela Duckworth, "Grit: The Power of Passion and Perseverance," TED, May 9, 2013, www.ted.com/talks/angela_lee_duckworth_grit_the_power_of_passion_and_perseverance; *Grit: The Power of Passion and Perseverance* (Scribner, 2018).

having stamina. Grit is sticking with your future, day-in, day-out. Not just for the week, not just for the month, but for years. And working really hard to make that future a reality. Grit is living life like it's a marathon, not a sprint."[2]

Build a Circle of Support

You don't need a lot of people, but you do need some of those replenishing relationships to hold you up and give you hope. Do you have replenishing relationships? Do you have a circle of support? A remarkable biblical account tells how that on one occasion when Moses and the Israelites were battling the Amalekites, as long as Moses held up the staff in his hand, the Israelites had the advantage. But Moses became tired and could no longer hold up the staff, so the Amalekites began to prevail. The friends and family of Moses found a stone for him to sit on, and they held up his arms until sunset, resulting in Israel winning the battle (Ex. 17:8–16). We all need people who will come alongside us. When our adult child has drifted and is wandering, having that support becomes crucial. Yet too often pride gets in the way and we feel ashamed to reach out for help. Hope isn't something that happens by chance—it's something we build with intention.

Here is one model that has worked for me. This is my circle of support.[3] It doesn't build overnight but is tested with time. It is a community of caring people from all walks of life

---

2. Duckworth, "Grit."

3. This phrase came from my podcast interview with Dr. Chinwé Williams and is also explained in her book *Calm, Courageous, and Connected: A Parent's Guide to Raising Emotionally Resilient Kids* (Orange, 2025), 81.

who help lift my hands and heart when I'm weary. Building that circle takes intentionality and purpose. I've never met anyone who says it isn't worth it.

Circle of Support

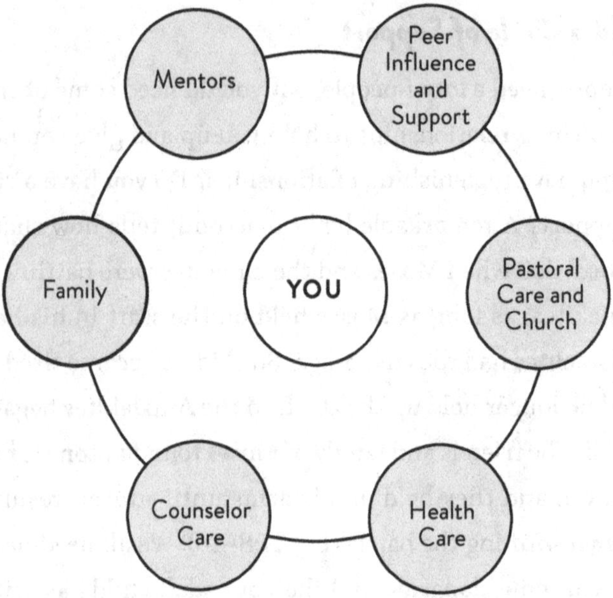

Mentors

Peer Influence and Support

Family

YOU

Pastoral Care and Church

Counselor Care

Health Care

Because doing life with adult children is a long-term process, it's not surprising that we become weary, especially if our adult child is straying. It's up to us to find our own individual support system. Some people find the notion of establishing a network for support, protection, and wisdom to be overwhelming at the start. One woman said to me, "I have no one in my life whom I can think of to be in my circle of support." You might feel the same way, so I don't want to make the process sound easy. Still, here are some steps you can take to start building this group who will stand beside you. Let me explain.

SEARCH OUT MENTORS

Do you have mentors you can turn to for wisdom? Often a mentor is not someone you have a formal relationship with but rather someone you know who is doing life well and you trust. Because Cathy and I were not raised in strong Christian homes, we had to seek out men and women who became mentors in the areas of marriage and parenting. When our kids reached adulthood and we felt completely lost, we invited an older couple we admire to dinner. We came armed with questions, and the practical tips they shared were real game changers.

As you think about finding a mentor, take a chance and invite someone you respect to coffee. What can it hurt? Listen to their story, ask questions, and you will undoubtedly be better off for it. This might sound a little odd, but some of the finest mentors I've had, I met in their books—some even after they had died. I call these people paper mentors. Obviously, you can't take them to coffee, but there is so much wisdom to be gained from people who write books.

CULTIVATE PEER INFLUENCE AND SUPPORT

Do you have replenishing relationships in your life? Sure, we all have acquaintances, but do you have friends with whom you can share your deepest thoughts?

I've been in a support group with six men for twenty-three years. We meet every Tuesday morning. I'm a better husband, father, and Christian because of these men. Cathy meets with a group of women weekly. In her group, there is lots of laughter and fun and sometimes a few tears. It is a safe place to share. When one of our daughters encountered challenges in college, the encouragement and wisdom from my support network were invaluable.

Do you have peer relationships that inspire you? Relationships don't just happen, you create them. They are cultivated through time and sometimes sacrifice. If you lack a group, I encourage you to seek one, or at the very least, find a friend who can offer meaningful support and become a means of replenishment.

RELY ON PASTORAL CARE AND THE CHURCH

As you can tell, I come from a faith-based background. For me, involvement in the church and a relationship with our pastors have been an important part of my support circle. Just this week, my wife and I shared dinner with one of our pastors and his wife. Moments like that remind me of how life-giving it is to be truly known and loved. There's also a teaching element in these relationships that can be a powerful source of encouragement. Over dinner our pastor shared that he spends twenty to thirty hours preparing his weekend message. His dedication shows and carries over into his relationships—he's a gifted communicator, and many weekends we leave with insights that, when put into practice, strengthen our faith, our parenting, and our marriage.

I encourage you to make your church part of your own circle of support. Too many people in the church suffer silently in shame if their adult children are struggling when it just doesn't have to be that way. The support is often there, but sometimes you must look for it. Don't expect it to be perfect. If you have had bad experiences in the church, don't give up. Not all churches are toxic or excessively judgmental. Find a church that is a good fit for you. At its best, the job of the church is to come alongside you and support you.

STAY PHYSICALLY ACTIVE AND HEALTHY

How is your health? Your body is connected to every part of your life, and if your body is failing, it affects everything else.

For example, my friend Bob boasted to me that he hadn't been to a doctor or dentist in nine years, and he did little to no physical activity. Not a good idea. A year later, his physical health fell apart, which affected his emotional health. His body was not able to handle the stress of his family problems.

As you think about your own health, get regular checkups and choose physical activity that works for you. You can't change the problems your adult child may be having or change some of their behavior, but you will want to be in good enough health to sustain your ability to take on some of that stress.

FIND A GOOD COUNSELOR

As I interviewed parents of adult children who had strayed, many said that the biggest help they got was from committing time—and yes, money—to counseling. Nothing shocks a good counselor. They are trained to understand patterns that you may not pick up. Even the Bible says, "Plans fail for lack of counsel, but with many advisers they succeed" (Prov. 15:22). If you haven't yet worked with a counselor or coach, consider adding one to your circle of support. Few resources can offer the kind of hope and insight they provide, especially when you are reinventing your relationship with your adult children.

PULL IN YOUR FAMILY

If you are fortunate to include family members or at least one family member in your support system, then you are most blessed. Your family member must be a safe person you trust and can confide in. Often with family the support can be a two-way relationship, which is a beautiful thing. When a family member is part of your support system, you have someone who truly knows you—your history, your strengths, and your weaknesses. They're often more willing to be honest about your shortcomings, yet they'll love you unconditionally. You may notice I didn't include adult children in this circle of support. While it's possible they could fill that role, it's not always the case. Adult children are rarely the best source of counseling, and it's wise not to expect a lot of emotional support from them. If you are among the fortunate few who do receive that level of care from an adult child, cherish it and be deeply grateful. For most parents, it's more helpful to seek encouragement from peers and mentors who share similar values and life experiences. Here's a thought worth holding on to: "When your child leaves home and their life fills up with fresh experiences, follow their lead."[4] Too often you can become trapped in a cycle of fear, control, emotional distance, and even panic. And in the process, you lose sight of your own well-being. It's time to break that cycle, and building a healthy support system will make a huge difference.

It is so much tougher to live life without a community of caring individuals around you. If this kind of support is lacking in your life, start working on it today by exploring these six steps. Remember, you are on this journey for the long haul.

Create a Welcome Mat Culture with Your Adult Child

Even when you are facing turmoil and tough times with your adult child, do all you can to make your home a place of peace, not a home with extra pressure. Be welcoming without hovering. As much as you can, stay involved and maintain a connection, even if it's not the connection you dreamed of when your child was younger. You can agree to disagree with their choices and still let them know you love and support them. Change happens when there is a relationship—one that is safe and welcoming. What is sometimes difficult but so important is that we will need to put out the welcome mat in principle—irrespective of outcomes. A young adult once told me that even while she was in full rebellion against her

4. Jim Burns, *Finding Joy in the Empty Nest: Discover Purpose and Passion in the Next Phase of Life* (Zondervan, 2022), 7.

parents' values, she still felt drawn to them. They continued to include her in every family gathering and never wavered in their love for her. She said they had a way of sharing laughter, activities, and family traditions—even while disagreeing with her choices. They were showing her that it's entirely possible to enjoy meaningful time with your adult child, even when you don't agree with their behavior. The key to keeping the relationship strong is to keep the relationship going. This often means reinventing the relationship, keeping your mouth shut, and not trying to fix everything. Since offering unsolicited advice is usually taken as criticism, one of the major disciplines for every parent of an adult is to bite your tongue. Don't say everything you think. Even if your actions are backed by pure motives, your adult child might still view your advice as a sign that you don't think they are capable. It's not your responsibility to fix your adult child. You don't have the power to fix anyone but yourself.

A welcome mat culture says that you lead with love and practice kindness even when your child is living contrary to your beliefs, values, and lifestyle. It also communicates that you are no longer responsible for your adult child's happiness. The moment you stop carrying the weight of making them happy is the moment both you and your adult child feel the freedom to develop a stronger bond. As you hand that responsibility back to them, you'll feel freedom, even in the midst of relinquishing control. A healthy relationship always says that good and hard can coexist. That concept gave Cathy and me a lot of hope when we needed it.

You Are Not Alone

Parents of adult children who have strayed and compromised their values or faith commitments frequently experience a profound sense of loneliness. But you don't have to be alone. There are books to help you and a circle of support to get you through the tough times. You can have hope. Sometimes there are beautiful stories of transformation like the story of Eric and his family at the beginning of this chapter. The fruit of "staying in the story" even when it is really hard is worth it. Sometimes the stories contain a twist of something exceptionally difficult. But again, good and hard can coexist, and your hope may not come all wrapped up nice and neat. It may be messy and awkward, but didn't someone once say, "It's not over till it's over"? And your story isn't over yet. You can reset the relationship with your adult child.

And one more thing. God loves and cares for you and your adult child with an unconditional and unfailing love. My personal experience is that parents of straying adult children who lean on the comfort of God do better. He walks with you through your journey, no matter what happens along the way. Here are a few promises from the mouth of God:

- "The Lord is close to the brokenhearted" (Ps. 34:18).
- "Be strong and do not give up" (2 Chron. 15:7).
- "'For I know the plans I have for you,' declares the Lord, 'plans to prosper you and not to harm you, plans to give you hope and a future'" (Jer. 29:11).

Never Give In, Never Give Up

In 1941 the great political statesman of Great Britain Winston Churchill was invited to speak to his old alma mater boys school. By that time, he was one of the most famous leaders in the world and one of the world's greatest orators. Academically, he had done very poorly and not thrived when he was at this school. But things had obviously changed. When he came to address the students, the atmosphere was electric.

Churchill approached the podium. The boys were sitting quietly and respectfully, ready to hear great words of wisdom. His entire talk was four minutes and forty-one seconds long. Who says you have to be long-winded to make a great point? A twenty-second part of that talk has been repeated millions of times. From the podium, Churchill looked into the eyes of each boy in that room. After a few brief opening remarks, he quietly said, "Never give in, never give in." Then he pounded the podium and at the top of his voice yelled, "Never, never, never give in!" He went on to say, "In nothing, great or small, large or petty—never give in except to convictions of honor and good sense."

He then walked off the stage and left the school as the students sat in silence pondering what he had just said. That was good advice in 1941, and it's good advice today. If we take Sir Winston's advice to heart with our adult child, it means never give in to despair, for there is hope. Never give in to fear, for living with fear will do nothing to help. Never give in to grief or shame, for it will only take you down. Your circumstances may not turn out the way you wanted or even prayed for, but by staying in the story and never giving up, you will find hope.

This book won't magically solve all the issues with your adult child, but it will show you something important: Parents who learn to thrive in these relationships often experience a shift in mindset. It's about facing the hard stuff with a new attitude. You really can find hope, even in the mess, when you understand that the good and the hard often come together.

CHAPTER 2

BE THE ADULT IN THE ROOM

You might be able to relate with Patty. She had pure motives and good intentions arising out of her deep love for her son and concern for the direction his choices were leading him. She could see the writing on the wall for possible negative consequences of his poor decisions. Adding to her distress, Patty didn't approve of his live-in girlfriend, and she strongly disliked the girl's mother, who seemed to encourage the poor choices they were making. Patty's family had money, and she suspected that the girlfriend's mother saw the relationship as the ticket out of poverty and debt.

Patty wanted to help, and she wanted the very best for her son. After all, she had been a guiding force in his life for more than twenty years. But here was the problem: In her desperation, she was parenting from a place of fear. Her approach—though well-intentioned—was dominated by negativity. It showed up as criticism, guilt trips, lectures, blame, and emotional pressure. Her desire to protect turned into control.

Patty's son showed me three texts. One to him, one to his girlfriend, and one to his girlfriend's mother. They were long, intense, emotional, and extremely critical. And of course, all three texts were shared with all the parties involved.

By the way, if you have something important and emotional to say, texting is a poor way to do it. It's incredibly difficult to have a respectful and constructive dialogue through texts—especially emotionally charged ones.

Here I'll summarize the texts to each person.

- To her son: "I can't believe you are throwing your life away. Your father and I have given you so much, and we have sacrificed our lives for you. You are ungrateful. You don't return my texts or phone messages. Why are you doing this to me?"
- To his girlfriend: "My son deserves better. You have taken him down a slippery road. I can't see how this is going to last."
- To his girlfriend's mother: "How dare you allow my son and your daughter to live together in your house? You are even charging him rent. I don't trust you."

Here is the deal: After speaking with both Patty and her son, it seems to me that she is probably right about many of the concerns she has, but she is addressing them in a way that's not very effective. Her son isn't showing the maturity of a responsible adult, but Patty needs a lesson in adult communication too.

If your adult child is straying, one of the most important decisions you can make is to "be the adult in the room." This means showing respect and developing connection even when you don't agree with their actions. This means not saying everything you think and carefully choosing how you share advice. It's your job to be the calmest person in the room even when you are screaming with fear and pain on the inside. Let's face it, fear leads us to make terrible decisions. Intensity, panic, and control also cause relationships to shut down. Guilt and obligation don't build genuine connection. "Word vomit" by you or your adult child does more harm than good in an already fragile relationship.

Many parents haven't learned how to parent an adult, and many adult children haven't learned how to behave like one. For parents, this shift demands both discipline and emotional self-control. Redefining how you engage with your adult child is not an easy task, especially when they have strayed from some of the family beliefs, values, or both. But this is where you have to take the lead. The moment you begin to make the shift from control to connection, something powerful happens—both you and your adult child are liberated.

That said, don't expect your relationship to feel immediately natural. I did my PhD work in Great Britain, and as an American, I found learning to drive on the "wrong side" of the road awkward, stressful, and honestly, kind of weird. But over time it became second nature and was fine. The same goes for this transition from control to connection. Here are four principles to guide you as you make that shift and move fully into your role as the adult in the room.

Principle 1: Embrace the Shift

When you transition from control to connection, your role changes from one of authority to guidance, offering support and wisdom. The goal is to move from being in control to being more of a mentor. Many parents struggle because they are still treating their adult child like they did when their child was younger. Part of being an adult, whether the child is doing a good job or a poor one, is taking charge of their own life. As parents, we spend nearly two decades in charge, and then we are fired as day-to-day parents. In the best of relationships, we move to mentor and influencer, but that transition depends on how we handle the shift ourselves.

Hailey and Peter learned to embrace the shift the hard way with their daughter. It was a shift they had to work at with each other and with their daughter. Both of them are amazing leaders in their church. Cathy and I love them and their children. When their daughter was ten years old, we could imagine that she was going to give them a run for their money. She was beautiful, strong-willed, and adventuresome. Hailey and Peter's dream for their daughter was to marry a youth pastor, be active in church leadership, and live nearby so they could be close to their grandchildren. That was not their daughter's dream.

At sixteen she told her parents she was staying with her best friend but instead spent the night camping at the beach with an older boy. At eighteen she moved across the country with a man who used drugs. After that relationship failed, she came home briefly, only to move out again, but this time with a woman a few years older, entering into a same-sex relationship. That relationship eventually ended, and she came back home, expressing a desire to get her life on track. Not long after, she married William, a previously married man with two children.

Needless to say, Hailey and Peter were heartbroken by the path their daughter had chosen. They argued and worked and exhausted themselves trying to "fix" their daughter. But the harder they tried, the more distant she became. Not only did their striving affect the relationship with their daughter, but it became the biggest source of tension in their marriage as well.

After going through some intense counseling—both for their relationship with their daughter and with each other—Hailey and Peter eventually came to a place where they could accept her decisions without necessarily approving of them. Things seemed better. They even laughed about their dream of her marrying a youth pastor. I remember them once saying about her current husband, "At least he only smokes pot and doesn't do cocaine or heroin like one of the other guys she dated." They had clearly shifted their expectations—significantly.

At first Peter didn't like the new pot-smoking husband. They had little in common. Peter admitted he was embarrassed by him. The young man had a low paying job, and Peter was put off by the extensive tattoos covering his arms, neck, and back. But he could also see that his daughter loved him. So Peter kept trying. He told me that his counselor asked him to write down all the things he liked or had in common with his son-in-law. Peter wrote:

- We both love Stephanie (his daughter).
- He seems to be a good dad.
- He hasn't kept her away from us.
- He smokes pot, but he refrains whenever he is around us.
- He is an avid fan of the Los Angeles Dodgers! (And so was Peter.)

Peter showed this page to me. He asked, "What do you think I should do with this?"

I said to my friend, "Sounds like you need to work on being grateful and take him to a couple of Dodger games."

Funny enough, it was the Dodger games that became the unlikely bridge. Long story short, Peter's son-in-law is now the youth pastor at his church. It's pretty incredible. He's still not exactly the guy Hailey and Peter imagined their daughter would marry, but over time their relationship has grown strong and genuine. And in a surprising twist, Peter even got a small tattoo on his arm. And the son-in-law gave up his addiction to marijuana.

As their story illustrates, when you let go of control and pursue connection instead, most adult children then have the opportunity to feel trusted and valued and not managed or guilted into relationship. They need space to make their own choices and sometimes make their own mistakes. Just like when they were little, our grown children tend to learn more from real-life experience than from our advice. The more we respect their independence, the more influence we actually gain. One of the great paradoxes of doing life with our adult children is that as we give our kids the freedom to fail, they grow up. They become more open to hearing our perspective because it's offered, not imposed.

Here is a phrase I've learned to use: "That sounds really hard." Then silence. Sometimes the adult child will ask for some advice and sometimes all they need is to feel heard. I heard someone once say, "Listen more and don't give advice unless asked. There is a reason you have two ears and one mouth." Or, as one of my favorite comedians, Jim Gaffigan, likes to say about the joy of parenting, "I feel like I am constantly correct and usually ignored." Embrace the shift from control to connection.

Principle 2: Lead with Love

Kindness matters. Lead with love even when you don't feel like it. "Choose love and move forward" is the phrase I say to myself, but that concept is easier said than done. I get my inspiration on this principle from none other than God himself. He is the greatest example of showing love and kindness even when we blow it. Throughout the Bible, we are reminded of God's unconditional and unfailing love.

God says to us, "I love you no matter how you are acting. Your actions and my love are totally different issues." This is the kind of love we are to show to our adult children. I can imagine God saying to you and me, "I know every sin in your life and every skeleton in your closet. I know your darkest thoughts, and I have a word for you: 'You are the apple of my eye.'" What an amazing thought: God loves us not for what we do but for who we are, his children. Romans 2:4 says, "God's *kindness* is intended to lead you to repentance" (emphasis added). As parents of adult children who have strayed, it's not easy to show love and kindness in the midst of their poor decisions or misguided beliefs. In the end, it may be our kindness that has the greatest impact on their willingness to change.

Remember, leading with love and practicing kindness doesn't mean we agree with our adult children's actions or encourage poor choices. There is such a thing as "tough love." Tough love means not being mean-spirited or condemning but rather allowing the natural consequences of poor decisions to unfold without bailing out our straying children. You can lead with love and kindness while still holding firm to healthy boundaries that build responsibility. It's possible to show empathy and practice tough love at the same time.

Acceptance doesn't mean approval. Acceptance says, "I love you where you are." We all have relationships with people who do things we don't approve of. Stay in the relationship with your adult child. When a mom or dad of an adult child tells me a story of violated values, I always ask, "Do they know what you believe? Do they know how you feel?" They always say, "Yes, of course." Then I say, "Stay in the relationship and grow it by being more than a one-topic parent."

I'm thinking of a young adult daughter and her mom who differed on many topics but found harmony by taking a cooking class together. One young man restored his shaky relationship with his dad by taking apart and rebuilding an old truck engine together. They still disagreed on some lifestyle issues, but their common ground was that old truck. And time spent on the project together made room for honest dialogue about some of the choices the young man was making.

When your adult child strays and violates your values, when the relationship is tense or strained, they still have one question for you—even if they have wandered a very long way: "Do you still love me?" And yes, it's possible to love them even if we don't agree with their choices. It's not always easy, but it *is* possible.

Principle 3: Improve the Relationship

Ask yourself, "Do I want to be right, or do I want to improve the relationship?" You can't have it both ways. Being the adult in the room is about more than being right. You might have the facts on your side, but if your tone is harsh or you get defensive, you'll still come across as wrong. Defensiveness shuts down connection. My dad always said, "Don't drown in shallow water." That is wise advice when it comes to being the adult in the room. When disagreeing with my wife or adult kids, I often ask myself, "Does it really matter?" Most things aren't nearly as important as we make them out to be. Some issues truly are critical, such as drug abuse, mental health struggles, or abuse. But casting a vote for a different candidate is not worth becoming estranged from your adult child.

If your adult child is deeply depressed and considering suicide, that's urgent—get them help. If they come home one day with a nose ring, that's probably not a hill worth dying on.

Being the adult in the room means knowing when to keep your mouth shut while still keeping the welcome mat out. If we were sitting together having coffee, you might notice I have scars on my tongue from biting it. Not really, but most of the time it feels like it. I'm the fix-it guy. I have good answers, and yet sometimes (or even often), I just need to let things go.

Ask yourself, "Am I willing to bite my tongue often?" You'll find it makes a difference. Here is another important question for you: "Am I offering words that heal or words that wound?" That answer will help you decide if you are focusing on the relationship instead of on being right. Making the shift from control to connection means not wasting your time on things outside of your power.

I could give you a long list of things that my adult children do that I don't think is in their best interest or a good long-term decision. You name the category, and I could show you my list. To be fair, even though I have those lists in my mind, my adult children are amazing individuals, and I'm deeply proud of them. But as they became adults and left the nest, they became their own people. Good for them. I don't want them to be clones of Cathy and me. However, I still have those lists in my mind. And that is where I need to keep them—to myself. If I start to offer unsolicited advice or criticize a decision, I listen to the bubble in my head that almost always says, "Stop it! Don't go there."

You might be completely right, but bringing up old wounds or personal hurts won't change your adult child's behavior. It may only create more distance than connection. You don't need to become a doormat—that's not it at all. But showing empathy and listening to your adult child will make a difference. Listening is the language of love and helps immensely to build a foundation for a healthy relationship in the long run.

More often than not, the most impactful adult in the room is the one who listens well. Even in silence, you are offering love and support. When emotions run high, choose to be the steady, calming presence. Resist the urge to interrupt or correct. Ask thoughtful questions rather than rushing to provide answers, even if you think you're right. Let them share their full story. Your silence and listening care can heal the relationship much quicker than any defensiveness you offer. Don't make your communication about winning the discussion. This is not about winning or losing an argument. It's about strengthening a fragile relationship that needs your maturity, integrity, empathy, and love. The sooner we realize that change won't come through criticism or negativity, the sooner we can offer something far more powerful through hope, connection, and trust.

I vividly remember an encounter I had with my daughter who had been in a relationship with a guy who, let's just say, was not my favorite. Frankly, he was a mostly nice young man, but I had some strong thoughts that he didn't treat my daughter very well. Life seemed to be all about him, and I thought she could do better. One night my daughter and I were out to dinner. She was telling me that she was thinking of breaking up. She did almost all the talking. I asked a few questions but mainly just listened and listened some more. At the end of the dinner, I had given her no advice, yet she said, "Dad, this has been great. You really helped me sort things out. Thanks so much for your insight." I had to smile because I really hadn't given her any of my "words of wisdom." She needed a safe place to unpack her thoughts, and I needed to keep my mouth shut.

Principle 4: Don't Be a Living Martyr

When it comes to her adult kids, Karla tends to be an *awfulizer*. I hadn't heard the term before my daughter Becca, who has a master's degree in clinical psychology, introduced me to the concept. It perfectly describes someone who immediately jumps to the worst-case scenario in their mind. An awfulizer is a person who imagines a situation to be as bad as it can be:

- "Our adult child hates me."
- "He will *never* have a healthy relationship with me."
- "She will *never* have a meaningful life."
- "He will *always* make bad decisions."
- "She will *never* grow up."
- "It's *always* going to be bad, and I'm going to die a sad person with no relationship with my kids, who won't ever visit me."

If you awfulize, your pattern of negativity might be the cause of trouble in your relationship with your adult child and the reason they keep their distance from you. If you are playing the living martyr role, it is not going to end well, because an unchecked critical spirit leads to bitterness. Living martyrs make life about themselves and their problems. They tend to focus on self-pity.

Strong negativity toward your adult child (or toward anyone else, for that matter) is destructive. Negativity kills relationships. Flee from it! Here is the apostle Paul's advice to a church in Greece: "Do everything without grumbling or arguing" (Phil. 2:14). Negativity can kill a relationship quicker than a wildfire. Flee from it. This may sound like an oversimplification, but negativity will devour the happiness of your relationship with your adult child like few other issues will. If you think pessimistically, you will view the world and relationships in a negative light. The Bible says, "As he thinks in his heart, so is he" (Prov. 23:7 NKJV) We become what we think about all day long.

In my experience, a healthy parent resists the urge to use criticism as a means of correcting behavior. Let me gently remind you that no one hears a constant tone of criticism. People tend to emotionally shut down—or even distance themselves physically—when they feel they are constantly being corrected or criticized. When we are feeling down about ourselves or unhappy, we often become critical of others. We have to curb what can become a habit of unchecked critical thoughts. The most powerful organ in the body is the mind, and it takes discipline to renew our minds for good. The Bible teaches us how to replace a critical mindset: "And now, dear brothers and sisters, one final thing. Fix your thoughts on what is true, and honorable, and right, and pure, and lovely, and admirable. Think about things that are excellent and worthy of praise" (Phil. 4:8 NLT).

We have a clear choice when it comes to how we react to our adult children's decisions and actions. We can awfulize and be like living martyrs, our mindset playing out the victim role, leading to more heartache. Or we can quit validating the victim mentality inside us and choose to "fix our thoughts" on what is good, which brings hope and helps us rise above our circumstances and be the adult in the room.

Here are four questions that may help you be the adult in the room:

1. Where have I put an emphasis on control rather than connection in the relationship?
2. What can I do in a practical way to pursue connection with my adult child?
3. Is there an opportunity to lead with love and practice kindness in our relationship?
4. In what areas of my life can I do better at biting my tongue and keeping my mouth shut?

CHAPTER 3

YOU ARE NOT DEFINED BY YOUR ADULT CHILD'S CHOICES

Pat and Marcia's son, Justin, was the youngest of four, and the only boy with three sisters. Pat and Marcia told me he was a joy to raise—easygoing, affectionate, and fun. After high school, he chose to attend the same Christian university as one of his sisters. But once there, he gravitated toward a wild, rebellious crowd. They were fun kids, but at age eighteen they were free from their parents' tight reins, and they put a lot of energy into experimental behaviors that weren't in alignment with their upbringing or the school rules.

By his second year of college, Justin was hooked on pot, which soon opened the door to other drugs and choices that strayed far from the values he was raised with. His grades suffered, and the four years it should have taken him to earn his degree stretched into six. While his parents were pleased that he graduated, they were deeply concerned that he was making some very bad decisions. Their concerns were justified. After he partied for a summer, they talked him into going to a drug rehab facility. He came out clean, and they came out $30,000 more in debt. He spent a year with YWAM (Youth with a Mission) in Hawaii, and his parents were thrilled. They had their son back. After that year, Justin returned home and began dating someone new. It wasn't long before the old familiar patterns began to resurface. Out of the blue, he told them he was moving from Nebraska to San Francisco with no job, limited funds, and no plan. He couch-surfed for a few weeks and found a job waiting tables. It didn't take Pat and Marcia long to piece things together—his new girlfriend, who wasn't on their "approval list," had made the move with Justin.

The next thing they knew, he was living with his girlfriend and another roommate. Although he wasn't estranged from his parents, he had left their values and faith behind—both of which he once held as his own. Pat and Marcia assumed the relationship with the girl wouldn't last since many of his other relationships had been short-lived. So when the announcement came that he and his girlfriend were getting married in Mexico in six weeks, they were taken by surprise. They attended the wedding, and as most moms can understand, Marcia figured out Justin and his girlfriend were pregnant even before it was announced.

Marcia told me that after the wedding ceremony and reception, which had much more of a party scene vibe than a celebration of commitment, she and Pat sat in their hotel room, held each other, and cried. She said, "Weddings are supposed to be happy occasions, but this was one of the saddest days of my life." She kept saying to Pat, "Where did we go wrong? Because he was our baby, we didn't give him good boundaries, and look at the mess we've caused. Even his sisters were disgusted with this wedding. I feel like a failure!" They were experiencing deep grief and taking on the blame.

Pat and Marcia were focusing on their adult son's poor choices that carried lasting consequences. But in their grief, they were taking far more responsibility than was truly theirs.

Pat and Marcia were good parents. They had built a good foundation for Justin to become a responsible adult, and Justin chose another path.

Here is what author Jill Savage has to say about kids who rebel and violate values: "If they decide to build a shack on the foundation you laid for them, your job is to pray they'll eventually tear down the shack and build a beautiful castle you laid the foundation for."

The Risk of Overthinking

Tearing down the shack and building a castle in its place is your child's responsibility, not yours. Yet many of us overthink the situation and take on the burden. Cathy and I have done that many times. Obviously, Pat and Marcia did too.

When we overthink, we often give ourselves too much credit for our adult child's failures and poor choices. The truth is that even good parents can have kids who make poor choices. It seems like every time one of our own adult children made a decision we didn't think was wise, we blamed ourselves. Cathy and I played the "shoulda" game. We shoulda been better parents. "We shoulda done this" or "We shoulda taught them that." We still struggle with this kind of wrong thinking.

If you hear yourself starting a sentence like Cathy and I have done many times, with "If only . . . ," then you are doing some destructive overthinking about your parenting. The shoulda game robs you of your joy. One of the key experts in working with parents of adult children is counselor Kathy

Cunningham. She said it best: "If you are feeling exhausted, overwhelmed, and defeated, remember that parenting is only hard for good parents." We can't be defined by our adult children's choices.

Do you overthink your adult child's issues? If you do, you have joined with millions of other parents who need a reset in their mind and actions. But here's the truth: You can't shift the mindset if you or your spouse keeps replaying your child's choices and carrying the weight of them as your own.

What is overthinking when it comes to your adult child? In its simplest form, overthinking is constantly worrying about and ruminating on your adult child and their decisions. Ruminating is rehashing the same things repeatedly, which is not helpful. A lot of worry focuses on future events. These events or worries can sometimes center around hypothetical situations that don't happen. Mark Twain said, "Worrying is like paying a debt you don't owe." Overthinking easily becomes detrimental to your emotional health and your relationship with your child. Overthinking to an extreme may be a symptom of generalized anxiety disorder (GAD), which is often associated with depression, anxiety, and even post-traumatic stress disorder. Yes, it's true, our adult child's behavior can even cause PTSD.

No matter the severity of your anxiety, here are a few signs that you are overthinking:

1. You're unable to think about anything else.
2. You become a one-topic parent.

3. You feel mentally and emotionally exhausted.
4. You fixate on things with your adult child that are out of your control.
5. You second-guess your parenting decisions of the past.
6. You can't stop worrying about your adult child's choices over which you have no control.
7. You constantly remind yourself of your mistakes in parenting or in life in general.
8. You spend time on the "what if" questions.

Generally speaking, there are at least three types of overthinking.

1. *All or nothing thinking.* This is where you see situations as black and white, either all good or all bad. I've heard parents say, "I'm a total failure as a parent. I invested my life in my kids, and I failed." When I talk with parents who feel this way, it's often clear that they have an overly negative way of looking at themselves. Although their child has chosen a path that doesn't mirror their views or values, it doesn't erase all the good they've done.
2. *Catastrophizing.* I introduced the word *awfulize* in chapter 2, and *catastrophizing* is a similar mindset. Awfulizing is the "underlying irrational belief" and catastrophizing is the "cognitive, behavioral, and

affective consequences of the belief."[1] This type of thinking—"Things are way worse than they actually are"—often means the parents are in an emotionally dark place. Catastrophizing and fear walk hand in hand. Fear can sometimes drive the relationship with their child, and the results are seldom healthy.

3. *Overgeneralizing.* This type of overthinking happens when you base a rule or expectation for the future on a single or random event from the past. You start to believe that it will "always" or "never" be this way. This leads to worrying about things that might never occur.

During a private conversation with Pat and Marcia from the earlier illustration, I shared the eight signs of overthinking and three types of overthinking. Marcia's response was, "I do almost all the signs. And is it even possible to have all three types of overthinking? You are living inside my head." Pat nodded and said, "If we could help Marcia get past some of this overthinking, I think it could really help our relationship with our son. I also think it would do wonders for our relationship with each other."

He was right. I had a ten-minute conversation that same week with their son, Justin. He told me that, yes, he had strayed

---

1. Scott Harris Waltman and Angelique Palermo, "Theoretical Overlap and Distinction Between Rational Emotive Behavior Therapy's Awfulizing and Cognitive Therapy's Catastrophizing," *Mental Health Review Journal* 24, no. 1 (2019): 44–50, https://doi.org/10.1108/MHRJ-07-2018-0022.

from his parents' faith and values. He even told me he knew he had made a lot of mistakes and wanted to change. He said, "If my parents weren't so consumed with all the things I have done wrong, our relationship would be so much better. I will never be the exact duplicate of them or my sisters, and their constant worry and grief over me is driving a wedge between us." He then added, "My wife is just over them. My mistakes are mine. I'm responsible for the mistakes, not my parents."

That's pretty insightful for a guy who is unfamiliar with the term *overthinking*.

A Healthier Way

I have a great deal of respect for Pat and Marcia. They didn't want to overthink their parenting history, and they refused to let Justin's choices determine their worth as parents. As they worked toward improvement, they asked me if I would meet with them a few times to explore a healthier way of dealing with these deeply rooted habits. I told them I would meet with them, but in a coaching capacity, not as a counselor. I told them, "I think I can help you move your mindset and reshape some of your patterns. It seems like you're stuck in a rut. It's going to take commitment, intention, and real effort on your part. Are you ready for that kind of work?" They seemed enthusiastic to get started. I shared this thought with them in our first meeting: "First, we form habits, and then they form us. Conquer your bad habits, or they'll eventually conquer you." I suggested three sessions where they would work on three different ways to communicate from a new mindset. I promised them that it would not be easy but very helpful.

Session 1: Reframe Your Mindset

In our first session, we focused on one simple but powerful exercise: Reframe Your Mindset. Like many parents, Pat and Marcia were stuck in negative thoughts that messed with every aspect of their reasoning and relationships. I gave them an exercise to help break that cycle. I sometimes call it What Else Is True?

Reframe Your Mindset Exercise

- Fact: Justin chose to live with and marry a difficult woman, and the reason they got married was because she got pregnant.
- What else is true: The baby girl is a beautiful gift from God.
- What else is true: Although they don't go to church, they asked one of Justin's sisters and brother-in-law, who are strong believers, to be their baby girl's godparents.
- What else is true: Justin wrote his mom a beautiful Mother's Day card and took her out for lunch.

After doing this exercise, Pat and Marcia had a meaningful breakthrough. They realized that their circumstances had not changed, but their attitude *could* change, and that makes all the difference in the world.

Try the Reframe Your Mindset exercise for yourself. In

what area of your relationship with your adult child could you apply this exercise? Take some time and work through it.

Session 2: Trust and Relinquish

The next session I did with Pat and Marcia was also relevant for me. Cathy likes to say, "Jim, we have a Messiah. He is doing very well; you don't need to replace him!" Similarly, Pat and Marcia struggled with the natural desire to step in and fix everything for Justin. They gave him a wonderful gift of paying for his drug and alcohol rehab, but it didn't work perfectly. Like all parents, they had to realize they couldn't rescue their son from every situation he got himself into. I taught them the prayer I often pray: "Lord, teach me to parent the children I have, not the kids I thought I would have." Trust and relinquishment don't usually come naturally—they require intentional discipline and focus. That's why the next exercise is such a valuable part of navigating life with your adult children. I've found the words and actions *honor* and *protect* to be especially helpful in fostering both trust and relinquishment. They seem to fit hand in hand.

Here is the exercise for session 2:

Honor and Protect Exercise

- Fact: Justin still struggles with sobriety. It seems he is getting better, but then at times, it's evident he is still using.
- Honor and protect: We will put our trust in God, and

despite Justin's actions, we will relinquish our will to God's will.

- Honor and protect: We will honor our commitment to tough love by allowing Justin's poor choices to bring him the consequences he needs to give him the best shot at returning to sobriety. At the same time, we will protect our hearts by getting some counseling and attending periodic Al-Anon groups.
- Honor and protect: We will continue to invest our time and love in Justin's wife and our granddaughter, and to witness to them. We will protect our hearts, which are so often breaking, and focus on doing the right next thing. With Justin and his family, we need to be strong cheerleaders with healthy boundaries.

Session 3: Acceptance Without Approval

This concept goes against the grain of our mindsets, especially with parents who do a lot of criticizing to correct behavior. In this session, we must learn to stay on our adult child's team. Even if you don't agree with their decisions, make it clear that your love is unwavering. Commit to creating a "welcome mat culture" that will make your home environment a place of peace, not pressure. You can welcome your adult child (with healthy boundaries) without hovering. Staying on their team means offering all the love and support you can without enabling unhealthy dependence or compromising your beliefs or morals.

Here is what the exercise for session 3 looked like in the Pat and Marcia story.

Acceptance Without Approval Exercise

- Fact: With Justin life is an emotional roller coaster. He is always a charmer with us, but that charm seems to mask dishonesty and inauthenticity. We grieve his actions and lifestyle, and we do not want our love and support to be mistaken for approval of his lifestyle.
- Acceptance without approval: We will respect the fact that Justin is an adult and has the freedom to choose his actions. We will choose to stay in the messy middle of loving him and creating clear boundaries that have his and our best interests in mind.
- Acceptance without approval: Even though we don't think Justin or his wife is parenting our granddaughter the way we would want them to, we remain committed to being her biggest encouragers and surrounding her with love. We will be "party-time grandparents" while doing our best to respect Justin and his wife as the parents of our granddaughter.
- Acceptance without approval: Justin and his wife know how we feel about their behaviors, and they know what we believe. Nevertheless, we will maintain a relationship that keeps us together in love.

No one will say these exercises are easy. Relationships get complicated and sometimes messy, but the purpose of exercises like these is to help parents understand that they can live in the messy middle and they are not responsible for their adult children's choices. And since you are not defined by your adult child's behavior; you can offer them the power of encouragement and belief.

Jesus looked at a disciple named Simon, and said, "'You are Simon son of John. You will be called Cephas' (which, when translated, is Peter)" (John 1:42). In the Greek language, Peter means "the stone" or "the rock." And although it took some years and a betrayal to get there, Peter (Rocky?) became the leader of the Jerusalem church. Peter became what Jesus called him to be. It's hard to encourage our adult children if we're constantly beating ourselves up or overanalyzing our circumstances. That mindset makes it more difficult to give them the space to make better choices and live out their true calling. When you stop defining yourself by your adult child's decisions, you gain the freedom to love and believe in them in a powerful way. As you overcome feelings of inadequacy and confusion, it becomes easier to connect with your child on a deeper, more meaningful level. But you can't do that if you stay trapped in self-blame over their choices.

Sam's Story

Dr. Sam is a loving husband and father and an excellent physician. He worked in a teaching hospital in Spokane, Washington, after spending much of his career as a missionary doctor in Kenya. Most days as Dr. Sam made his rounds, a handful of medical residents and students trailed behind him as he taught them the art and science of practicing medicine. With Dr. Sam, the students always knew they were learning not only the best medical practices but also important practical life lessons as well.

One evening while making his rounds with his entourage of medical students, Dr. Sam visited a young woman who was in the hospital again for a drug overdose. They all knew her as a "frequent guest" in the emergency ward from numerous overdoses. She also happened to be the daughter of one of Dr. Sam's fellow physicians.

That night when the young woman came in, she was very sick, and thanks to Dr. Sam and his team's expertise, her life was saved. The following day, Sam and his team returned to check on her. They were skeptical of this young woman ever changing. As they were getting ready to leave the room, she looked into Sam's eyes and said something to him that she had said many times before: "Doctor, I'm going to quit taking drugs; I'm going to pull my life together." Sam smiled at her and simply said, "I believe you."

When they left her hospital room, the medical students asked him why he would say, "I believe you." She had said she was going to quit using many times before yet always came back high on drugs.

Sam looked at them and said, "Love believes all things and hopes all things. What good would it do if I told her I didn't believe her?"

Ten years later, Sam and his wife, Judy, were at a large

social gathering. A radiant young woman approached him and said, "I don't expect you to remember me, but ten years ago you told me you believed in me to get off drugs. I could tell you really did believe in me. I have been sober for most of those ten years. I'm happily married, and I have two beautiful children." With tears in her eyes, she gripped his hand and said, "Thank you for believing in me."

That's what the power of belief can do. As parents, when we avoid taking on excess responsibility for our adult children's choices, new opportunities open up and allow us to find freedom and joy in the relationship. This empowers us and our adult children toward better connection and ultimately less heartache and more hope.

CHAPTER 4

LEARN TO LIVE ABOVE YOUR CIRCUMSTANCES

This might sound trivial to some people, but it drives me crazy when my adult kids ignore a phone call or don't respond to a text promptly—especially when I know they're free. I'm not even sure if any of my three wonderful daughters have ever actually listened to voicemail. After I have left a long, lengthy phone message, if they return the call, they usually start out with "What's up, Dad?" I used to ask if they listened to the voicemail, but I've stopped. I already know the answer: "No, I didn't listen. What's up?" Then I remind myself of how when I was in college, in the ancient days before cell phones and internet, I'd call my parents collect on Sunday afternoons, but sometimes I'd forget—and weeks would pass without a call. I want my kids to respond to me within ten minutes! I know there are much bigger problems with adult children than not answering a text, but I've learned a good lesson through this process. There is a direct correlation between how I am doing with my emotional, physical, and spiritual health and how I perceive my relationship with my kids.

The more emotionally healthy and secure I am, the easier it is to navigate life with my adult children. When I'm in a good place emotionally, I don't take things so personally. If they don't call, don't visit, or forget to send a card on my birthday, in my "good zone" I realize it's not about me; they are just living their lives. It doesn't mean they don't love me, it simply means they were so caught up in their own stuff that they forgot. When I keep things in perspective, I realize it's not the worst thing that could happen to me.

Here is a phrase I use a lot in my own self-talk: "Your circumstance may not change, but your attitude can change, and that makes all the difference in the world."

A friend of mine recently met with her daughter-in-law. Their relationship had been rocky at best. My friend had lost access to her son and grandkids because the daughter-in-law blocked most connections. My friend needed to understand that this relationship will be a lifelong one and that access to her son and grandkids will be primarily through this daughter-in-law. My suggestion to her was not to come to the meeting with "guns loaded" but rather make the meeting all about the daughter-in-law. I suggested to my friend, "It's important to hold back and not say everything you think. Focus on listening." If the daughter-in-law opens up about anything she's struggling with, offer her support. Let the conversation center on her experience and not your own.

If you happen to be facing a similar story, try to avoid criticizing to correct the behaviors. You might want to point out how wrong your adult child is and how right you are. Those conversations may come later, but you are in it for the long haul, so don't make the first meeting about any of that. There is a reason for her distancing, and perhaps through building the relationship you can find some answers.

Laying a Firm Foundation

To move forward in a meaningful way, we have to rise above our family situation and focus on becoming the healthiest version of ourselves. The more emotionally healthy and grounded you are in the relationship, the more room it creates for the other person to grow and respond in a healthier way too. Do you know what the most well-known sermon of all time is? Even people who don't usually pay much attention to sermons say that Jesus' Sermon on the Mount is one of the most powerful messages they have ever read. Jesus gave this message more than two thousand years ago, and it still inspires, challenges, and provides great advice today. At the end of the sermon, he summarizes his message in three sentences: "Anyone who listens to my teaching and follows it is wise, like a person who builds a house on solid rock. Though the rain comes in torrents and the floodwaters rise and the winds beat against that house, it won't collapse because it is built on bedrock. But anyone who hears my teaching and doesn't obey it is foolish, like a person who builds a house on sand" (Matt. 7:24–26 NLT).

Jesus was saying that rain, wind, and storms will come to our lives. It's a matter not of if but when. The strength of our foundation directly influences how we navigate life's challenges, especially in the relationships with our adult children. If we build our lives and homes on the bedrock, storms will come, but our foundations will remain. If we build our lives and homes on sand, the storms of life will easily overwhelm us.

My friend Kay Warren had a son who committed suicide. I can't think of a more tragic experience for a mom or dad. In reflecting on her journey, Kay shared, "Someone recently asked me how I survived my son's suicide. I told him, 'I sent my spiritual roots deep into the character of God for more than fifty years. Circumstances tried to brutally rip out the "tree" of my faith—but the roots held.'"[1] Kay has been incredibly transparent and honest about her deep pain. Her circumstances didn't change. They were awful. But the foundation she had cultivated in her life enabled her to persevere one day at a time.

There are no shortcuts to becoming grounded and establishing a firm foundation. It takes time and discipline, but it is worth it. Author John Ortberg has a famous phrase that has found its way onto posters and memes: "Love God and do the right thing." I told him recently that I changed his quote. I added, "Love God and do the right thing and repeat daily for the rest of your life!"

We can rise above our circumstances, but it requires hard work and focus. By making intentional, wise decisions in our own lives, we become stronger and more prepared to face the challenges that come our way, especially within our families. When you prioritize your own spiritual, emotional, and relational growth, rather than focusing on your adult child's lack of growth, your stability will become a powerful example for your family.

---

1. Kay Warren, *Choose Joy: Because Happiness Isn't Enough* (Revell, 2020), 65.

I mentioned something similar to some parents who were deeply struggling with their adult son. The dad said, "So in other words, you are telling us to 'get a life.'" I smiled and replied, "Yes, I guess I am. One that is healthier so you can better handle whatever is being thrown at you." I told them, "When I'm in a healthy place, not a perfect place, but good, I don't automatically assume my adult child's distance is rejection of me."

Psychologist Henry Cloud once told me, "I cannot blame them for what I do with what they do to me. I am responsible for how I respond." That's good advice. When you have built a strong foundation, you begin to realize that how your adult child is treating you is a reflection of them and not you. By contrast, your response to their treatment is a reflection of you.

Before Freedom Comes Pain

Rising above our circumstances often starts with doing internal work in our own lives. If we carry unresolved pain and don't deal with it, we tend to repeat the very patterns we want to escape. I tell people all the time, "If you don't heal, you will repeat." It's like the definition of insanity—doing the same thing over and over, hoping for a different response. Unresolved grief leaks out. Unresolved past relationships leak out, and patterns resurface in our relationships. The question is: What will it take for you to become emotionally, spiritually, and relationally healthy enough to build a solid foundation for your own life? The hard truth is we often know what needs to change but don't act on it. We won't have a perfect problem-free life this side of heaven, but most of us can move in a better direction.

Cathy and I came from somewhat dysfunctional families. We met in college and got married right after her graduation. We quickly realized that we were going to need to work on "our stuff" or the marriage was not going to last. We also knew that if we had kids, we would likely repeat the negative family patterns of our past unless we made a conscious choice to change. One year into our marriage, we were faced with a decision: recover or repeat our family history in the way we did life. The choice to change turned out to be one of the most important of our lives.

During that time, we put two words together: *transitional generation*. Yes, it's possible to break the cycle and change the trajectory of your family, but only if you are willing to do the hard work. The principle I mentioned in chapter 1, "We face either the pain of discipline or the pain of regret," became a key for me to become the person to break the chain of dysfunction in our family. Part of my journey to recover and not repeat my negative family patterns was to quit blaming Cathy for all our issues and look at my own issues. After all, when I was pointing a finger at her, three fingers were pointing back at me. The only person I could truly change was me. That meant getting ruthlessly honest about my own brokenness in order to heal. The pain of discipline works with our mindset just as well as with other aspects of our life.

Now as a counselor of sorts to other parents, I see often that when just one person gets healthy, it moves the needle for the family in a good direction. Breaking the chain of dysfunction in your family starts with you. You will need to focus on healing from your own emotionally unhealthy relationships.

When your children become adults and live with their own set of values and experiences, a new season begins for you as well. While writing *Finding Joy in the Empty Nest*,[2] I noticed a pattern among the people I spoke with: Those who invested in their own personal growth began to thrive. They found renewed purpose and meaning through such things as participating in a women's Bible study at their church, joining a gym, volunteering at a hospital, or investing in building deeper friendships. Some went back to school or found a new job.

The ones who didn't work on their own emotional, spiritual, and relational health were the ones who struggled the most to find meaning and joy in their new life without kids in the home. Many parents who had devoted their lives and energy to raising their children struggled as empty nesters because they weren't willing to make healthy adjustments in their own lives. Without those changes, they often experienced deep sadness, depression, and anxiety when their children moved on. For many of these parents, their lives began to feel empty and even bitter. A coffee shop in San Diego has this sign out front. "Life is too short to be bitter." I know they are talking about coffee, but isn't that true of life

---

2. Jim Burns, *Finding Joy in the Empty Nest: Discover Purpose and Passion in the Next Phase of Life* (Zondervan, 2022).

as well? There is no benefit to a parent harboring bitterness in their heart for whatever circumstances come their way.

Isolation Is Not Your Friend

Healing doesn't happen in isolation. To rise above your circumstances, you must invest in relationships that replenish and encourage you. Who inspires you? Who motivates you to be the best person you can be? Who is the person you enjoy spending time with? Invest in those kinds of relationships. When you surround yourself with replenishing relationships, you are moving toward a foundation for emotional and relationship health. This thought goes back to chapter 1, where we discussed creating your own circle of support. Your own healing will often come through connection, support, and even your vulnerability with people who love and support you.

You don't need to be part of a big group to keep from isolation. For example, my wife, Cathy, is an introvert. She is great with people, but she doesn't need a crowd. She enjoys one-on-one coffee times or taking a walk with a friend. Do whatever keeps you from being isolated. Who sees you? Who knows you? How is your circle of support? Initiate and be intentional about developing friendships.

Cathy and I love watching movies. Cathy is usually the last one out of the theater because she likes to stay until the last credit rolls. It used to bug me, but now I'm used to it. Who are the "rolling credits" in your life? Who cheers you on, holds you up, and helps you move forward? One woman recently told me that life with her adult children is hard. But once or twice a week she gets together with friends who encourage her, and that small investment is what gives her strength to go back into the battle of life with her adult children. Smart woman. She is nurturing her own emotional growth with the community she is building around her. It's making a difference.

Adaptability Is Key

When an adult child has strayed, a healthy relationship is difficult—if not impossible—without adaptability. I like what Martin Luther is credited with saying: "You cannot keep birds from flying over your head, but you can keep them from building a nest in your hair." Adaptability doesn't mean that you let your adult children walk all over you. It does mean being willing to adjust your expectations, dreams, and relationships.

This all goes back to being careful that you work on your negativity pattern. Adaptability and negativity do not work well together. We all have problems and patterns. Problems can be solved. Patterns, however, are a bit tougher. They have already become ingrained behaviors that are harder to break, especially if they are rooted in negativity. Identifying your negative patterns will help you break them.

Understanding your triggers is crucial to maintaining good mental health and navigating the complex terrain of dealing with our emotional lives with our adult children. At its core, a trigger is anything that elicits a specific response.

As a parent, I had to learn about my negativity triggers

to become more adaptable. The recovery community uses the acronym HALT to describe four common triggers: hungry, angry, lonely, and tired. If I am experiencing any of these, I know I need to take care of the triggers before I try to solve the bigger issue.

What are your triggers? Name them and it will become easier to be adaptable and flexible in a relationship with your kids, or anyone else for that matter. I have a friend who always says, "Hurt people hurt people." That makes sense, and the good news is that we can move toward a healthier way of living. Don't expect this to happen overnight. We take steps in the right direction, and sometimes those steps are baby steps. As Henry Ford once said, "Nothing is particularly difficult if you divide it into small steps."

We've been talking about negativity, but the same practice works for developing a positive mindset. We need to limit exposure to our triggers. I do this through a daily discipline of journaling my prayers and feelings. I also do it by practicing what I call "thank therapy." Most mornings I make coffee and sit in my chair near our back yard. I spend about twenty minutes reading the Bible and a devotional book, and I journal. I always include a list of reasons why I am thankful. This thank therapy always seems to straighten out my attitude.

Thankfulness helps to vanquish depression and anxiety and reminds me how fortunate I am. Thank therapy is especially helpful if, during a relational issue, I find reasons to be thankful for the person who is annoying or frustrating me. It doesn't always fix the problem, but it almost always gives me a better perspective.

Try this little exercise: Put down this book and write twenty reasons why you are thankful. See if this practice can't become a habit that makes a difference in your life.

Setting a Healthy Tone and Atmosphere

Dr. John Gottman, one of the world's leading experts in relationship research, introduced a concept called the "magic ratio."[3] Gottman found that for a relationship to thrive, there needs to be five positive interactions for every one negative interaction. He found that people with that kind of interaction had successful marriages. In fact, he has never seen a marriage with that ratio end in divorce. Amazing!

If we apply the magic ratio to our relationships with our adult children, the dynamic is shifted to the positive. And yes, sometimes we need self-discipline and maturity to keep our mouths shut. Rachel Wolchin said it best: "Maturing is realizing how many things do not require your comment."

I have a friend who met with her adult child who had been incredibly difficult. She went into the meeting with understandable hesitation. However, she decided to keep the conversation focused on her daughter and as positive as possible. She wrote me this note after the meeting: "I took much of your advice to stay in the story and keep it about

3. Kyle Benson, "The Magic Relationship Ratio, According to Science," Gottman.com, October 4, 2017, www.gottman.com/blog/the-magic-relationship-ratio-according-science.

her and not about how she had hurt me. She was sweet, kind, and open. I didn't understand much of her perspective, but it's hers, not mine. Listening to her and being positive toward her has reset our love for each other. With God's help, I stepped over my own needs to allow her to have space. It felt wonderful! I met a new version of her today." Wow! That's what I'm talking about.

Larry Senn authored a wonderful book a few years ago called *The Mood Elevator.*[4] It helped me understand how to set a healthy tone for my life. He wrote from a business perspective, but it helped me from a personal growth and relationship point of view. Here is what he calls the mood elevator:

High mood states: grateful, wise, insightful, creative, innovative, resourceful, hopeful, optimistic, appreciative, compassionate, patient, understanding, sense of humor, flexible, adaptive, cooperative, curious, interested

Lower mood states: impatient, frustrated, irritated, bothered, worried, anxious, defensive, insecure, judgment, blaming, self-righteous, stressed, burned-out, angry, hostile, depressed

We have a choice to live in the lower mood state or the higher mood state. People who live in the lower mood state will not thrive in their relationships with their adult children

---

4. Larry Senn, *The Mood Elevator* (Berrett-Koehler, 2017).

or anyone else. Our goal is to spend more time in the higher mood state. We don't get there by wishing or hoping; we have to be intentional and put forth real effort. But the payoff is more than worth it. To spend time in your higher mood state, you first need to know what helps you get there. What simple practices lift your spirits? For my wife, it's exercise, coffee with a friend, or tackling a lingering chore. For me, it's reading a good novel, going on a walk with my wife, or enjoying gelato. Everyone is different, but dwelling on our problems won't get us there. What works for you? Keep it simple and within reach.

Changing Your Parenting Perspective with Your Adult Kids

Someone has said, "Parenting is watching your adult children do weird stuff and telling your spouse, 'That definitely came from your side of the family.'" I know, it's funny, but it's not good parenting advice. Once our kids grow up, we need to relearn how to parent. What worked for us during our kids' childhood and teen years doesn't translate into the adult years. Kathy Cunningham shared a graphic that beautifully captures this shift. She called it "Counter-Intuitive Behavior for Parents of Adults That Can Actually Strengthen Your Relationship."[5]

Yes, as difficult as it is, we release our adult children in

5. My three favorite counselor resources for adult children who stray are Kathy Cunningham (aseedofhopecc.com), Tina Gilbertson (tinagilbertson.com), and Joshua Coleman (drjoshuacoleman.com). Check out their resources and counseling options.

Counter-Intuitive Behavior for Parents of Adults That Can Actually Strengthen Your Relationship

DO THIS	TO GET THIS
Give space	to build closeness.
Have hard conversations	to cultivate connection.
Be vulnerable	to strengthen relationship.
Encourage independence	to gain interdependence.
Let go	to hold on to what matters.
Accept change	for a strong relationship.
Listen	to be heard.
Give freedom	to build a strong foundation.
Practice self-awareness	for mutual understanding.

Kathy Cunningham (@kathycunningham717), "Counter-Intuitive Behavior for Parents of Adults," Instagram, February 22, 2025, www.instagram.com/p/DGX9OI_ucaz/.

order for them to become their own people, even when we don't agree or their values differ from ours. You can't manage their lives or carry them on your back. It isn't God's design, and it doesn't work. Their choices are now their choices, and they need to own those choices. This doesn't mean we stop caring. It means we stop controlling.

If your relationship with your adult child feels like a mess right now, lean into God's compassion and strength. You may say, "I'm in a mess." God says, "I'm good with messes. I can live with messes, and I can help." He may not take all your messes away, but he does promise to walk with you through them—especially as you work to adapt and rise above your parenting circumstances. Recognizing God's willingness to join you in your journey is the start to trading your heartache for hope.

CHAPTER 5

SETTING BOUNDARIES AND FOSTERING A GOOD RELATIONSHIP WITH YOUR ADULT CHILD

Tom and Kelsey are a great couple. I would call them model parents. They raised four daughters who were popular in school, active in youth group, and all-around awesome kids. Three of the four daughters drifted from their family's traditional values during their college years. Their twins were especially rebellious, fully immersed in sorority life, partying heavily, experimenting with drugs, and being sexually active. One day the girls called to ask if they could bring some friends home for the weekend. Tom and Kelsey were ecstatic—finally a chance to meet the people their daughters were spending so much time with.

When they arrived, it quickly became clear that these weren't just casual friends, but "friends with benefits." The twins had brought their boyfriends, along with another couple. Later two more guys showed up from their friend group to join the weekend gathering.

Tom and Kelsey's home was spacious, and with the other two daughters already living out on their own, there was plenty of room for guests. The bonus room above the garage provided the perfect spot for the two late arrivals. Things seemed to be fine at first. The young adults lounged by the pool, enjoyed snacks, and drank a lot of beer. It wasn't until much later, when Tom and Kelsey were past ready to go to bed, that they realized the couples were all planning to spend the night together in each of the available rooms. Tom and Kelsey had assumed guys would be sleeping with guys and girls with girls.

They were frustrated with their daughters for not addressing the sleeping arrangements earlier. They were also disappointed with each other because it hadn't entered their minds that the twins would go against the family values in their own home. They knew the girls were sleeping with guys at school, but they expected their daughters to abide by the family rules at home. Clearly their daughters had other plans—and hadn't thought it necessary to mention it to them. Tom and Kelsey sat in their bedroom trying to decide what to do. They felt torn. They had wanted to be seen as "fun, easygoing" parents, but they also had values in their home that they expected to be honored.

Finally, they decided Tom would walk out to the bonus room where most had congregated. They were cuddling and watching a movie. Tom looked at his two daughters and then made a general announcement. "Kelsey and I are going to bed. It's so good to have everyone here this weekend. I wanted to say that there are plenty of beds and towels, and we thought the guys could sleep in the back bedroom and the girls could all sleep in the twins' room. Oh, for you two guys who came in later, there's plenty of space in the room above the garage with a bathroom if you'd prefer that."

Tom told me you could feel the tension in the room, especially from his two daughters, who were mortified. Tom just turned around and walked back into his and Kelsey's bedroom.

Tom told Kelsey, "I'm not sure that went very well with the girls or anyone else."

The next morning, they were up early making pancakes, and as everyone came into the kitchen, it seemed like the group had respected the sleeping arrangements. After breakfast, their daughters announced that the group had decided to leave early and go camping at a state park on the beach. The girls asked if they minded if the two guy friends who came late could stay the extra night in the room above the garage. Tom and Kelsey said there was no problem with the guys spending the extra night.

Deep down, they were disappointed. Their idea of what was going to be a really fun weekend was now crushed, and it was obvious their plans were very different from the plan their daughters had in mind.

Before the gang left for the camping trip with all of the family's camping equipment, Tom and Kelsey asked their daughters if they could have a word with them. The conversation unraveled almost immediately. The daughters were angry. "Dad, you humiliated us in front of our friends. We are adults; our bodies and our choices are ours. You had no right to separate us like we were at a junior high sleepover. We are through with you forcing your rules on us. Plus, you wouldn't let us sleep in the same room as our boyfriends, but you had no problem allowing our two gay friends to sleep in the garage room together." Tom and Kelsey were stunned. Yes, their girls were adults, but this was still their house and their rules. And Tom and Kelsey were still paying for their daughters' college tuition, car insurance, and family phone plan. The girls left without saying goodbye, as if they were trying to punish their mom and dad. And of course, Tom and Kelsey were left with the mess in every room and the two gay guys, who were already sitting by the pool enjoying the extra night in the bonus room.

Although this isn't your exact story, what can be learned from this experience? I've heard versions of this scenario over and over through the years. Much of what went wrong in Tom and Kelsey's story might have been avoided if they had communicated beforehand and established healthy, loving boundaries. Too often, parents and their adult children fail to share expectations, only to find themselves in difficult situations. Setting healthy boundaries should be seen as a proactive choice—one that can prevent bigger problems down the road.

Establishing Healthy Boundaries Is a Very Good Thing

Sometimes establishing boundaries with our adult children seems so "un-family-like." Some might think it doesn't sound like a good relational decision. People have told me that having boundaries with their adult children sounds selfish or they fear that it will hurt their children's feelings. I think they might be missing the truth. Healthy boundaries in any relationship are more often than not a good thing. It takes time and energy to establish them, but they provide important guidelines for a healthy relationship.

Hindsight is always twenty-twenty, but let's look at how Tom and Kelsey could have used some boundaries to shape a better weekend with their girls. Boundaries are the ground rules, the playbook on which healthy communication is established. Sometimes we just need to get more information. Kelsey could have asked, "Who's coming?" When she found out both guys and girls were coming, she could have easily said, "Great, that sounds like a fun group. We will buy some snacks—what would you like? Maybe we can grill in the back yard. Just a reminder—same policy as when you were younger, the girls and guys will need to sleep separately. You know the drill—our house, our rules. Will that work for everyone?"

By communicating expectations ahead of time in a kind but firm way, Tom and Kelsey could have made the weekend more of a success. Communicating expectations early often prevents confusion or conflict later on. Someone has said, "To be clear is to be kind."

It's possible to set boundaries with your adult children with love and respect. And if you haven't been much of a boundary setter, you may feel guilt, worry that you are being selfish, or fear that setting boundaries will damage the relationship. They may push back, but when you set healthy boundaries up front and not in the heat of the battle, it is always better. Your job is not to make your children happy; that is their responsibility. Your role is to stand firm with your own values without trying to control theirs. When you live with healthy boundaries, you stand firm, love deeply, and set those boundaries wisely. When you consistently hold to those boundaries, even in times of disagreement, you send a clear message that you are respecting your children as adults but also respecting yourself.

A few weeks later, once things had calmed down after some ugly texts from the twins, Tom and Kelsey were able to connect with their girls in a calmer environment. The parents did a great job of reestablishing the relationship. Tom led out by apologizing to his girls. "Mom and I are very sorry the weekend turned out like it did. We should have let you know ahead of time that we haven't changed our thoughts on the rules in our home. We didn't ask who was coming, and you didn't tell us. That's on all of us. We love you and always want the best for you."

Leading with an apology and showing some empathy was a good thing. They weren't wrong in establishing their "our house, our rules" policy, but notice that they didn't escalate the issue by immediately blaming the girls. If I had to say who was primarily at fault, I'd say it was mostly the girls for not telling their parents the plan for the weekend. There is no doubt they knew how their parents felt and what they believed. The result is that the apology caught the girls off guard and they responded with softness and accountability of their own. So much of dealing with boundaries is the manner in which we handle them. Clarity with kindness. Strength with compassion.

As Tom and Kelsey began to understand that they were not the source of their adult children's happiness or responsible for their girls' lives, they found it easier to love them while establishing guardrails in the relationship. They realized they were watching some of the poor decisions of the daughters play out before them without dealing with any boundaries.

One morning Tom and Kelsey met for coffee with their notebooks in hand. They talked through boundaries around topics like finances, time, sexuality, substance use, school, and expectations. The conversation wasn't perfect—these rarely are—but by the end, they had a clear set of intentional decisions and boundaries laid out. They were already halfway there, knowing that eventually they would need a family conversation to share these thoughts with their daughters.

They followed through a few weeks later. Tom and Kelsey met with their daughters, speaking with love and kindness while truly listening to their concerns. They handled some difficult moments without becoming defensive. Tom described it as the closest he had ever experienced to an adult-to-adult conversation with his girls. I had shared one of my favorite phrases with him: "I respectfully disagree." He applied the phrase, because there were some issues where the only option was to agree to disagree—simply, calmly, and with love.

Respecting Their Boundaries

When setting boundaries with your adult children, it is important to remember that respect goes both ways. This is not a one-way street. Our daughter Becca is probably the best example of someone who handles boundaries with maturity and grace in our family. After she graduated from college, she moved to Ecuador for a year to work with young girls through a mission organization. When she returned to the States, her former roommate had moved out, so Becca asked if she could move home for a few months as she pondered her next move. We were thrilled to have her.

I decided to practice what I preach and have a conversation about boundaries and expectations. Cathy and I prepared well in advance. We sat down over Becca's favorite meal, and I pulled out my notes, which usually earns me eyerolls from all three of my kids. We kept our expectations simple. We asked for one shared dinner a week. We asked that since her hours were different than ours that she would give us a quick text around 11:00 p.m. if she'd be out late. That worked most of the time. I also handed her a bucket with bathroom cleaning supplies, including a toilet brush, and asked her to keep her bathroom clean, along with a quick lesson on the proper use of a toilet brush!

Then off the top of my head, I asked her, "Do you have any expectations of us?" She thought for a few moments and said, "Yes." To be honest, I wasn't expecting that. "Dad, when I have friends over and we sit in the family room or out in the back yard, you just come and invite yourself into the group. I'd rather you not do that and wait until I invite you." Yikes, I had no idea it was a social miscue. I may be old, but I'm still a youth pastor at heart. I love students, and I felt it was natural to jump into their conversations. I thought for about five seconds, wanting to get defensive, but bit my tongue and said, "Becca, thank you for letting me know. I am so sorry for doing that in the past, and I'm glad you let me know." What a great lesson from my daughter. Case closed.

As you think about your own adult child, you may not be thinking about a boundary as small as Becca's request to me. But they matter. You are in this relationship building for the long haul, and often when adult children see their parents honoring boundaries, they begin to soften theirs. Boundaries go both ways.

Almost daily I hear from parents who are deeply hurt by their adult children's boundaries—especially children who have deconstructed their faith. Some parents are told not to talk about God or not to take the grandkids to church. My heart breaks for them, but I remind them gently, "You are no longer the parent. Respect the child's request, even if you disagree with it."

The Benefits of Boundaries

Living with well-communicated expectations can bring health to the relationship with your adult child. Healthy boundaries, when expressed with thoughtfulness and care, open the door to honest communication—even when there's disagreement. This brings a mutual respect between you and your adult child. It gives you a chance to honor their independence even if you disagree with their actions. With boundaries you can parent by responding in love rather than reacting in defensiveness or anger. With boundaries it's easier to say no when needed, especially around sensitive topics like finances or lifestyle.

Sean Part 2

In *Doing Life with Your Adult Children: Keep Your Mouth Shut and the Welcome Mat Out*, I introduced the readers to Sean. He was a smart, handsome, and winsome college graduate who was failing to launch well. He walked into my office with his parents, who looked tense and exasperated. Sean was charming, relaxed, and in control. Since graduating from college, Sean had moved back home and, for more than three months, had slept in until 1:00 p.m., partied at night, and continued to use his parents' credit card. His mom still made his bed every day and cooked him a vegan meal while she cooked a different meal for her husband and herself. At one point in the conversation, Sean's mom looked at me, pointed at Sean, and yelled, "Sean has a problem." I replied, "Actually, I don't think Sean has a problem." I remember everyone looking at me puzzled, including Sean. "I think you two have the problem." I added, "Sean is getting a pretty sweet deal." That opened the door to a hard but honest conversation about enabling behavior and the need for boundaries if he was going to thrive. That conversation was six years ago.

To the credit of both Sean and his parents, they put together some boundaries, expectations, and an action plan to help Sean launch into responsible adulthood. The launch was not without some bumps and misfires.

Recently, after several years, I decided to call Sean's parents to see how he and they were doing. His mom said she appreciated the call, and that Sean happened to be at their house with his wife and new baby. It sounded like he was doing well, so I asked if I could speak to him. I asked how life had been in the last six years. Here is what he said: "At first I hated the boundaries and the action plan we put together. I was comfortable and enjoying life after graduation. But in my heart of hearts, I knew it was good for me. I did get a job. I hated it. I quit and found another. I moved out with a friend, met my wife—she's an all-star—and she actually brought me back to church. Now I'm working with her dad in the family business. I get along great with my parents. Those boundaries and expectations were not what I wanted, but they were what I needed." He then added, "I love my life right now." That was a far cry from the young man who left my office in a huff six years earlier. I believe that without those boundaries, Sean would not be in such a good space in life.

Codependency and Boundaries

I can't write about healthy boundaries without also talking about codependency. Since I come from a family where alcoholism was present on both sides, this means I've not only observed alcoholic behavior but personally experienced codependent behavior. Many parents who struggle to set boundaries with their adult children often find themselves caught in some form of codependent behavior at some level.

Forty years ago, Melody Beattie wrote a book called *Codependent No More.*[1] This book was written out of her own experience as the wife of an alcoholic. Her book influenced

1. Melody Beattie, *Codependent No More: How to Stop Controlling Others and Start Caring for Yourself*, revised and updated (1986; Spiegel and Grau, 2022).

the world on the pitfalls of codependent behavior. Her definition of codependency was that it was a behavioral condition in which people prioritize the needs of their loved ones ahead of their own, often at the expense of their own needs and feelings. She was one of the first to say that codependent behavior not only is unhealthy but is a serious barrier to creating connection and closeness.

Here are some of the characteristics of codependence with an adult child:

- excessive control
- excessive caregiving
- poor boundaries
- low self-esteem
- driven by fear
- always attempting to rescue
- being manipulative, often indirect manipulation
- denial that they are practicing codependency
- undisciplined words and actions
- enabling

One mom, who I assumed was very codependent in her relationship with her son and who truly wanted him to pull it together, asked, "Is it possible to love too much?" The answer isn't simple, but the truth is that not everything we do in the name of love is actually helpful. The word *caregiving* is a beautiful word of love and service, but when lived out in an unhealthy way, it becomes obsessive and hurts relationships.

In their book *Boundaries*, Henry Cloud and John Townsend tell the story of a loving dad who only wants the best for his son. All of his attempts at caregiving, enabling, and control are driven by his fear that his son is failing. Henry points out to this dad that his approach is not working—it is enabling. Henry clarifies the situation, saying, "As it stands now, he is irresponsible and happy, and you are responsible and miserable." The father questions Henry, asking, "Isn't that a bit cruel, just to stop helping like that?" Henry's response is brilliant: "Has helping him helped?"[2]

That's the question we need to ask when supporting an adult child who has gone astray: "Are the ways we've been helping actually helping—or are they causing more harm?"

During my first week of graduate school at Princeton, I ran out of gas. We had just moved into our apartment, and I didn't know anyone. I wandered around looking for help and found a custodian in the basement. I asked if he had a gas can. He said he had one. He came back and said, "You are in luck, it has gas in it." I saw this as a gift from God. I poured the gas into my car. It started and then sputtered, and the engine died. I mean it literally died, because the gas he gave me was diesel and it damaged my engine. The custodian felt bad, and I had to call my dad for a loan to get the engine fixed. That experience taught me that good intentions aren't always the best solution to a problem. I rarely question the desires or intent of a codependent parent—they mean well, and they

2. Henry Cloud and John Townsend, *Boundaries* (Zondervan, 2017), 25.

want to help, but out of their own unhealthiness, they can cause more harm than good.

Here is a simple codependent relationship quiz. This is not a formal diagnosis tool—it's just another way for you to consider whether you have some codependent tendencies.

CODEPENDENT RELATIONSHIP QUIZ

1. Do you have a tendency to ignore or minimize your own feelings?
2. Do you often do things for your adult child that you really don't want to do just to make your child happy?
3. Do you have an excessive need to make your adult child happy?
4. Do you tend to sacrifice and neglect your own needs and desires?
5. Do you have an excessive need to get approval from others?
6. Do you tend to apologize or take the blame to keep the peace and avoid conflict?
7. Do you have excessive concerns about your adult child's habits or behaviors?
8. Do you experience guilt or anxiety when doing something for yourself?
9. Do you take on more work than you can handle to lighten your adult child's load?

How did you do? If you marked yes for more than three

to five of these questions, you have some codependent behaviors. To be honest, I found codependent behaviors in my own life, not just with my adult kids but in other relationships as well. We are all a work in progress, but this may help you to reflect on your parenting style or consider getting some support through counseling or coaching.

Self-Control and Self-Care

What are the practical implications of this chapter for you? Maybe you're starting to recognize where clearer and healthier boundaries are needed. Or maybe you're seeing that you've been carrying burdens that aren't yours to bear. Maybe you sense a nudge to invest more intentionally in your own personal and spiritual growth like we talked about in chapter 4.

We must learn that we cannot solve problems that aren't ours to solve, that worrying about our kids doesn't help, and that trying to fix things out of fear often makes matters worse. The Bible calls self-control a fruit of the Spirit. Sometimes codependent behavior becomes inextricably entangled with being a good Christian wife or husband, mother, or father. And that doesn't work out very well. By contrast, when I am focused on my own growth and learning self-control, I begin to respect my adult child's boundaries and am less driven to control or rescue them. When I am being undisciplined with my desires to control, I find great help in praying one of the most popular prayers ever written, "The Serenity Prayer." There are different versions of this prayer, but this is one I like: "God grant me the serenity to accept the things I cannot change, courage to change the things I can, and wisdom to know the difference."

Caring for yourself is not selfish—it is the very best gift you can give to those you love. As one adult child son said to his mom in my presence, "You are responsible for you, and I am responsible for me." It's not easy to take care of ourselves, and it's impossible to take care of all the needs of our adult children. Don't put off your self-care. I agree with Melody Beattie when she says, "Taking care of myself is a big job. No wonder I avoided it for a long time." When we approach life from a healthier mindset and lifestyle, the result is that we set healthy boundaries, which equals a better relationship with our adult children. Now is the time to set those boundaries. Not later, not someday. It's time. It's the pathway to hope and healing.

CHAPTER 6

THE DECONSTRUCTION OF YOUR ADULT CHILD'S FAITH AND WHAT TO DO ABOUT IT

In recent years, there has been a significant increase of young adults distancing themselves from the church, traditional faith and values, or both. Watching them disconnect from their spiritual roots is shocking and disheartening. According to the Barna Research Group, 64 percent of young adults leave the church after high school.[1] But emerging research is offering a hopeful perspective: Many who stepped away from their faith are beginning to return, even if slowly and quietly.[2] For many parents of adult children, however, that return hasn't yet happened—and may never happen. The pain is still real, the wounds are festering, and they have a sense of agonizing defeat.

Over the years as I've interacted with countless parents through my ministry, this issue of adult children leaving their faith prompts more questions than all other subjects combined. At speaking events around the globe, on my podcasts, and on social media, I field near-constant questions on this topic.

Many parents who raised their children in the Christian faith are caught off guard when those same children, now

---

1. "Church Dropouts Have Risen to 64%—but What About Those Who Stay?" Barna Group, September 4, 2019, www.barna.com/research/resilient-disciples/.

2. "New Barna Data: Young Adults Lead a Resurgence in Church Attendance," Barna Group, September 2025, www.barna.com/research/young-adults-lead-resurgence-in-church-attendance/.

adults, begin to deconstruct their beliefs. They assume the kid who was active in church as a child and as an adolescent will carry that same faith into adulthood. But for many families, that is not happening.

Our daughter Christy wrote a regular column for her university newspaper, and in her final column before graduating, she wrote, "I had to disown my parents' faith to own my own faith." That phrase was healthy on several levels, but hearing that she had to "disown our faith" sent us into a season of deep reflection—prompting us to question so much about how we raised her. We wrestled with regret and had deep anxiety over what was happening beneath the surface. We questioned everything about the decisions we had made in our family, as if her faith journey depended entirely on us. We knew the right things to say to others, but this was personal.

I remember a woman asking me during the time our kids were beginning to question their faith, "How long will it take for my son to regain his faith?" All I could honestly say was, "We never know." We have to stay in the messy middle. Some of our adult children live in the margin of faith for a long time, while others return with a newfound robust faith as they become mature adults. Regret can't rewrite the past, and no amount of anxiety will change the future. But love, patience, and presence matter in the middle of it all.

If your adult child has drifted from the faith, you are not alone. Countless numbers of parents carry the same pain and wonder, "Where did we go wrong?" Just this week, I've received questions from parents walking this road: "How do

I positively influence my child who doesn't believe in God anymore and barely wants a relationship with me?" "My son and his wife forbid me to talk about God to my grandchildren, and when they spent the weekend, I was told emphatically not to bring them to church. What should I do?" "How do I continue to love an adult daughter who was the leader in her youth group but now, after college, constantly talks trash about the church and her once strong faith? Her words are so very hurtful to me." Maybe you can identify with some of these questions.

What Is Deconstruction?

Deconstruction is a difficult word to define, given that people use it to mean different things. But in its most advanced form, deconstruction can feel like the death of a person's belief in God or belief in the church. When an adult child is deconstructing and rejecting their faith, the death affects them as well as those loved ones who still hold that faith. For parents especially, a sense of helplessness pervades their lives. Every interaction becomes strained, and if this rejection of the adult child's faith is not talked about, there is still the elephant in the room. Many parents who try to reassert their faith on their deconstructing child find out that approach rarely works. In fact, it can push the adult child farther away. There are better and healthier ways to handle the deconstruction of their faith.

Deconstruction has both a good and a difficult part. Some people call the good part "reformation," and I find that term hopeful. That's what happened with Christy. She didn't abandon her roots; she *reformed* her faith into her own. And what we now see is a vibrant ownership of her faith that doesn't mirror her parents' faith in every detail. The fruit hasn't fallen too far from the tree, for we attend the same church, attend family camp together, and share a deep living faith. However, in her reformed faith, she doesn't necessarily vote the same way as her parents do (I think we canceled out our votes in a recent election). We aren't in agreement on every point of theology, but it is a joy to watch her live out her faith through her actions in a fresh and beautiful way. The reformation process reminds me of a rosebush needing to be pruned. In winter it can look like death, but in the summer it resurrects and blooms with even greater beauty.

Christy's reformation was more of what we call *spiritual individuation*. *Individuation* is a term that psychology uses to describe the healthy process of a child moving from dependence to independence. It's the process of becoming a separate identity. The child still loves their mom and dad, but they are their own person. This is a necessary and healthy step to becoming a responsible adult. When the same process happens spiritually, we call it *spiritual individuation*, and we must look at that as extremely important and healthy. As a child, your son or daughter absorbs and reflects your faith, your prayers, and your church. But as they mature into adults, they need to form their own personal faith rooted in their own relationship with God.

The most painful part of watching your adult child deconstruct their faith is when there is no visible sign of return—when they seem to have completely rejected the beliefs that are central to your life. This can feel like a loss not only of your shared faith but also of moral and lifestyle alignment. Yes, it's complicated, but don't give up. Your spiritual discipline of relinquishing your will to God's will is a key component to remembering that when it comes to faith, he is in charge and his love knows no limits. As C. S. Lewis said, "The great thing to remember is that though our feelings come and go, God's great love for us does not. It is not wearied by our sins, or our indifference; and, therefore, is quite relentless in its determination that we shall be cured of those sins, at whatever cost to us, at whatever cost to Him."[3]

Six years ago, I created something for my book *Doing Life with Your Adult Children* that I have now shared with parents hundreds of times. I call it "the anatomy of an atrophied faith." Sometimes I use the words *lost faith*, for I believe that for our adult children to reclaim their faith, we must understand what caused their loss of faith in the first place. Sometimes a single event causes them to walk away from their faith, but I'm convinced that a lot of adult children drift away.

Here are six contributing factors to their loss of faith:

1. *Neglect.* When they become young adults, they simply stop practicing the spiritual disciplines of fellowship (community), Bible reading, prayer, worship, and generally being in touch with God. Neglect starts with

---

3. C. S. Lewis, cited in "What to Do When Your Adult Child Is Deconstructing Their Faith," *Focus on the Family*, February 29, 2024, www.focusonthefamily.com/parenting/what-to-do-when-your-adult-child-is-deconstructing-their-faith/.

small compromises and gradual abandoning of habits that once nourished their faith.

2. *Drift.* If they neglect their faith, they tend to drift away. But other factors can also cause drift. Sometimes the young adult doesn't even realize they are drifting until one day they realize God isn't as important to them as when they were younger. My dad was a farmer before I was born, and he would talk about cows grazing on grass, keeping their heads down and moving from one mound of grass to another, not paying attention to where they were going. They would look up at the end of the day and be lost. I think that happens with some adult children. They would still claim in the drifting stage to be followers of God but find themselves a bit lost and unsure how to find their way back.
3. *Unbelief or lack of trust.* For young adults who don't flex their spiritual faith muscles, those muscles atrophy and unbelief creeps in. With unbelief we often see compromise of values, morals, and thinking that may directly contradict what an adult child once believed. This can be a complicated experience because, although some leave because of their drifting, others develop a lack of trust or unbelief because of spiritual abuse, deep disappointment in the church letting them down, or lack of morality or integrity in the leadership of their church. One young adult told me, "I want to believe, but when one of our youth leaders attempted to seduce me, I shut

down my relationship with God. I can't get past the hypocrisy of my church." Now this doesn't mean that all churches are toxic, and it's important to note that each negative experience is not only complicated but deeply personal. Parents shouldn't be too quick to judge at this stage.

4. *Disobedience.* Disobedience is the natural outgrowth of the first three factors contributing to the loss of faith. This may be the first visible sign of change you see. All of us are disobedient at times, but here I'm speaking of a willful lifestyle choice in opposition to God's principles. Jesus gave a remarkable statement about this recorded in John 14:21: "Whoever has my commands and keeps them is the one who loves me. The one who loves me will be loved by my Father, and I too will love them and show myself to them." This is an insightful thought, because we find that God reveals himself to people through our love and obedience. This means that our adult child's disobedience—even if it is born out of pain and suffering—makes it harder for them to recognize God's presence in their life and his work in the world.
5. *Insensitivity to God.* The Bible calls this being "dull of hearing" (Heb. 5:11 NKJV). When a person is insensitive to God, the natural response is to harden their heart toward the Lord and his will for their life.
6. *Forfeiting spiritual purpose.* In this final stage of losing or dropping faith, the person tends to live with the consequences of choices resulting from forfeiting God's

presence and purpose in their life. This is heartbreaking for parents of adult children who remember them being passionate teens and now they are MIA with their faith.

When young adults describe what has caused them to wander from their faith, they don't necessarily include the contributing factors I've listed. This six-point sequence is meant to be only a general look at loss of faith. Every person has a different story and different experience. Parents and leaders in the church must be careful not to categorize each person—it's just not that simple. Because a crisis of faith is often self-defined, we need to take a step back and listen well. Young adults often point to real and painful reasons that have caused them to be disillusioned with Christianity.

Interestingly, many young adults who leave the church still have a high regard for Jesus. They are not surrendered to his will, but they don't seem to throw out the baby with the baptismal water. Jesus often gets high marks while it's the church and some of its teachings that mainly bug them. Here are some of the words and phrases I hear most often:

- The church is too political and aligned with Christian nationalism.
- The church is homophobic.
- The church practices old school misogyny and is patriarchal.
- The church is racist.
- The church is anti-science.

- The church is shallow.
- The church is exclusive.
- The church lacks tolerance.
- The church has repressive rules, especially around sexuality.

I love the church. But I can understand where this generation of deconstructed young adults get their criticisms and misunderstandings. Yes, there are churches and leaders out there who distort the gospel. There are churches who are as dysfunctional as any family. However, there are also beautiful, life-giving churches offering authentic faith. Somehow we need to allow our wandering adults to vent but, whenever possible, agree with them while still being an authentic representation of the love of God. Many of those disengaged with the church aren't really turning their backs on God as much as wrestling with deep wounds, harsh judgment, or even broken trust with spiritual leaders.

Rachel Held Evans was a prophetic voice for a younger generation of people who had been strong in the church until she became disillusioned with the American church. Rachel passed away at a young age. At her passing, she was still disillusioned. Although we wouldn't have agreed on every theological point, she made a very important statement for parents with adult children who are straying from faith: "I am convinced that what drives most people away from Christianity is not the cost of discipleship, but rather the cost of 'false fundamentals.'" She went on to say, "It's time we stop trying to 'set the world straight' by shouting out answers . . . and instead begin to follow Jesus on the path he walked—stepping into the lives of others through authentic care, deep listening, and honest, humble questions."[4] I think Rachel was onto something. We won't win them back through shame, guilt, or anger. Madeleine L'Engle summarized what we need to do and be for this generation: "We do not draw people to Christ by loudly discrediting what they believe, by telling them how wrong they are and how right we are, but by showing them a light that is so lovely that they want with all their hearts to know the source of it."[5]

You don't win an argument with someone who is deconstructing. You love them toward change by consistently loving them and making your light shine bright. That's it. The answer is showing your kids an authentic faith that stays true to your biblical convictions and loves unwaveringly with patient listening and a faith that radiates Christ.

Who Are These Wanderers?

Although every person who wanders away has a unique story about straying from faith, David Kinnaman categorizes what he calls the "dropouts" into three groups.[6] In the following, I borrow his labels and share his thoughts. You will probably find your son or daughter as either a nomad, prodigal, or exile.

---

4. Rachel Evans, *Evolving in Monkey Town: How a Girl Who Knew All the Answers Learned to Ask the Questions* (Zondervan, 2010), 207.

5. Madeleine L'Engle, *Walking on Water: Reflections on Faith and Art* (Convergent, 2001), 122.

6. One of the best books on why and how young adults are leaving the church is David Kinnaman, *You Lost Me: Why Young Christians Are Leaving the Church . . . and Rethinking Faith* (Baker, 2011).

Nomads

The nomads are on a "slow fade" from active faith. They have strayed. They most likely do not go to church on a regular basis, but they would still consider themselves Christians. Some of these nomads would tell you that they believe they will probably reengage once they get married and start a family. The nomads are usually not angry or hostile toward Christianity; they are just disengaged for the time being. Often, in their minds, participating in a faith community is optional. Sometimes nomads pick and choose what parts of the Bible they will follow. The third president of the United States, Thomas Jefferson, created his own Bible. He literally cut out parts he didn't like. Likewise, nomads "pick and choose" what Scriptures they feel are important and which to ignore.

Prodigals

The prodigals no longer describe themselves as Christian. They have been "deconverted." They would label themselves atheists, agnostics, or what is now commonly described as "nones." Many in this group left faith and the church because of a real or perceived bad experience. Some left for intellectual reasons, political disagreements, or moral conflicts.

Roger was a worship leader who moved in with his girlfriend right after getting his master's degree. During his last years in grad school, he was living a dual life, torn between his Christian faith and a lifestyle that went against biblical teaching. He was partying on Saturday night and leading worship on Sunday morning. He came to a moral crossroads:

He would return to living out his faith or change his beliefs to match his behaviors. My pastor, Jeff Maguire, has said, "Whenever beliefs don't match behaviors, people change their beliefs to match their behaviors." Or to put it another way, "Whenever morals do not match actual behavior, people often modify their morality to accommodate their behavior." That was Roger's story. He chose to quit believing and left his faith behind. Many other adults have done something similar.

Exiles

Exiles still believe in Jesus but feel alienated from the church. They feel torn between real world culture and the church. As they entered adulthood, they didn't feel at home at church, but they didn't want to leave it either. Many exiles want the best of both worlds. Kinnaman describes them this way: "They are skeptical of institutions but aren't fully disengaged from them."[7] I describe exiles as having one foot inside the church and one foot outside. One exile I know confessed to me that he felt like an outsider looking in. He said, "I want to belong. I want to join in, but something keeps holding me back."

Exiles, nomads, and prodigals all have different stories, so there's no one-size-fits-all explanation for where they are and how they got there. But the state of contemporary discipleship is definitely one factor among many. Research shows that when healthy faith conversations take place in the home, there is a greater chance that children will remain in the faith.

---

7. Kinnaman, *You Lost Me*, 77.

If you didn't have faith conversations much in the home, you don't need to beat yourself up—the home plays a significant part but not the only part in a person's faith development.

One of Jesus' parables was about a farmer who sowed seed (Matt. 13:1–23). The seed fell on four types of soil:

1. *The path.* Birds came and ate the seed.
2. *The rocky places.* The seed sprang up quickly, but the soil was too shallow for the seed to take root.
3. *Thorns.* The seed grew, but thorns choked the life out of them.
4. *Good soil.* The seed produced a good crop with a huge harvest.

In three of the four places the seed fell, it didn't make it. In the rocky soil, the seed didn't develop roots like it did in the good soil. Research tells us that the current generation of young adults lacks a deep understanding of their faith. The Barna group reported that only 4 percent of Gen Z has what is considered to be a biblical worldview.[8] Shallow soil doesn't produce healthy fruit. When teenagers and young adults have shallow soil and the Word can't take root, it is easy for them to shape Scripture into a more comfortable version. Like Thomas Jefferson, they tend to take some parts of the biblical narrative as true and ignore other parts. They shy away from God as the master designer. The wit of Mark Twain seems to make

8. Jonathan Morrow, "Only 4 Percent of Gen Z Have a Biblical Worldview," Impact 360 Institute, accessed October 9, 2025, www.impact360institute.org/articles/4-percent-gen-z-biblical-worldview/.

a lot of sense: "God created man in his own image and man, being a gentleman, returned the favor."

Five Things to Do When Your Adult Child Is Deconstructing

So what can we do? Fortunately, there is a lot we can do to stay in the story with our kids and their faith or lack of faith.

Here are the five things you can do when your adult child has deconstructed or is deconstructing.

1. Maintain a Climate of Openness and Grace

When you want to preach, lecture, judge, or shame, don't. Stay calm and stay engaged in your adult child's story. Remember, it's a marathon, not a sprint. Relationships thrive in an atmosphere of trust and compassion. Be consistent with your love, grace, and witness. Your actions will speak louder than your words. The apostle John gave some great advice when he wrote, "Dear children, let us not love with words or speech but with actions and in truth" (1 John 3:18). Take a deep breath, choose kindness over control, and bring grace to the relationship whenever you can.

2. Recognize That God Is Sovereign and You Are Not

If you are anything like me, you believe that God is in control and that he knows what he is doing, but it is a constant struggle not to want to fix the situation and take back control. I challenge Christian parents to practice the spiritual discipline of prayer and relinquishment of their adult children every day. Not only are you experiencing the power of prayer on a regular basis, but God, the creator and sustainer of life, encourages you to come to him in prayer. Our sovereign God promises, "'For I know the plans I have for you,' declares the LORD, 'plans to prosper you and not to harm you, plans to give you hope and a future. Then you will call on me and come and pray to me, and I will listen to you. You will seek me and find me when you seek me with all your heart'" (Jer. 29:11–13). These amazing three verses remind us that God listens, he has a plan, and he can be trusted. So again, it's always better to pray and not panic.

3. Accept Doubters

If your adult child is living with some doubts about God, that is not necessarily a bad thing. It can be a doorway to deeper belief. Be a safe place for your adult child to bring up doubts and questions. A couple who is involved in leadership with HomeWord[9] asked me if I would be willing to meet with their adult son whom I had met a few times. He was bright, fun-loving, and, according to them, had a lot of questions and doubts about faith. I know they were hoping I could "straighten him out." We met for coffee, and I said, "I understand you are dealing with some questions and doubts about your faith. I actually think that is a really good thing." He looked at me like I had just told

9. HomeWord is the family ministry I founded forty years ago. Our values are strong marriages, confident parents, empowered kids, and healthy leaders. You can check out the ministry at HomeWord.com.

him I lived on Mars. I added, "What's up?" He mentioned he was struggling with the concept of evil in the world. I paused for longer than comfortable. I answered, "That is one of the same questions I have been thinking about for a very long time. I've read experts' opinions on it, but I honestly still wonder sometimes about it." How's that for expert advice on my part? I don't think that was the answer his parents were hoping for.

We went on to talk about other issues, mainly about how it is very possible to be a Christian and realize you have questions and even doubts, but that is okay. I'm not sure that after that one conversation he went to work for a vital ministry, but I did tell his parents that their son needed a safe environment to doubt, search, and ask questions. Young adults are far more likely to return to faith if they feel free to ask hard questions without judgment. As David Kinnaman, president of the Barna Group, says, "I believe unexpressed doubt is one of the most powerful destroyers of faith."[10] Asking questions and having doubts is not bad; suppressing questions is.

4. Avoid Unnecessary Regret

Most parents of adult children who stray from faith at one time or another blame themselves unnecessarily. When each of our daughters had moments of not wanting to go to church, we would sometimes say things like, "We never should have gone on the family vacation and missed the youth group mission trip for the kids." "We should have prayed more with the girls."

---

10. Kinnaman, *You Lost Me*, 192.

We verbalized by blaming ourselves for their spiritual choices. Many parents spend too much energy self-blaming and wallowing in their regrets. I distinctly remember a Sunday morning when one of our daughters who was living with us while going to grad school calmly informed us that it was such a beautiful day that she was going to the beach with some friends instead of going to church with us. I made a passive-aggressive comment to her and immediately realized it was a bit out of line for an adult child. It would have been fine if she were in junior high, but not for a wonderful young woman. Immediately I was filled with regret and self-blame not only for the decision she made not to go to church but also for the way I reacted.

That evening when our daughter came home, she asked, "How was church?" I looked her in the eyes and said, "I am so sorry I made a smart remark to you this morning. Please forgive me." Her response was classic: "You raised me to make good decisions on my own. You did a pretty good job. Now you and Mom will need to let me decide when and where I go to church." Then she gave me a hug. I guess I'm still learning about setting boundaries and respecting my daughters' boundaries, as well as not blaming myself for every decision they make that I don't agree with. My experience says that much of the regret we have with raising our kids is unnecessary regret that clouds our thinking and reactions.

5. Continue to Influence Your Adult Child

You can be your adult child's greatest support even when your heart is breaking. Be there. Don't enable them, but being present in your child's life in a positive way matters more than you know. I call it "the power of being there." Younger children view your presence as a sign of caring and connectedness. It's the same for adult children. They may not want to spend as much time with you as you want to spend with them, but presence and support can come from offering a listening ear or sending them a note with a Starbucks card in it. But if you do anything, make sure it's connected to compassion, empathy, and kindness whether or not they are following your journey.

Your adult children. They love the church, leave the church, and sometimes find it again. Your acceptance of them does not equate with your agreement with their choices. When they have an "interrupted faith," one of the most difficult things to do is to show respect for them and for their freedom to choose what they will do with their faith. Oftentimes adult children will come back because they see their parents' light shine, or they will be drawn back because they miss the authentic community they once had at church. The great writer and thinker Frederick Buechner said, "Faith is homesickness." Pray for your adult child to have a healthy dose of homesickness that will slowly guide them back to faith.

CHAPTER 7

ESTRANGEMENT FROM YOUR ADULT CHILD AND HOW TO HEAL

It was only after I joined the New Life Live Radio team that I did much thinking about estrangement. New Life Live[1] is the largest Christian counseling broadcast in the world, and listeners call in to share a wide range of personal struggles. When I'm on the show, we frequently receive calls about problems with adult children. Estrangement from an adult child is one of the most common topics, often marked by deep sorrow, confusion, and sometimes anger.

As I began researching the issue of estrangement, I was surprised to discover that recent studies show that approximately 27 percent of Americans report being estranged from a family member.[2] Estrangement is most common among adults ages eighteen to twenty-nine. *Time* magazine calls this generation the "epidemic of estrangement." The article puts the blame primarily on the political climate in America. Some estrangement does come through political differences, but there are certainly other pathways to broken family relationships. Joshua Coleman outlined several key pathways to estrangement in his book *Rules of Estrangement*.[3] Among the ones that stand out are these:

---

1. New Life Live Radio has more than two million listeners each week. Get more information at newlife.com.

2. Marie Morin, "Mental Health Impact of Estrangement," Sixty & Me, October 13, 2022, https://sixtyandme.com/estrangement-mental-health/.

3. Joshua Coleman, *Rules of Estrangement: Why Adult Children Cut Ties and How to Heal the Conflict* (Harmony, 2024), 30.

- divorce—most often with the dad
- difficult relationships with in-laws
- mental illness or addictions, either on the part of parents or the adult child
- sexuality choices and gender identity issues
- feeling smothered by parental control
- disagreements over choices, values, or lifestyles
- and surprisingly enough, through a therapist's suggestion

There are certainly other reasons for estrangement, but these seem to be the most significant.

Friends in the counseling field have told me their counseling load with estrangement cases tends to spike around major national elections. One young adult told his parents, "If you vote for Trump, we are done." And he meant it. And a dad warned, "If you don't vote for Trump, I'm taking you out of my will!" And he meant it. Yikes! Usually there are other "stories behind the story," but estrangement seems to be the easy way out, quite similar to past generations turning to divorce without ever trying to reconcile or seeking help. Regardless of the primary issue, estrangement brings lots of emotions and pain—deep-rooted pain.

Navigating estrangement is extremely challenging. Any parent in this situation must swallow their pride and let go of the need to be right. Yes, you read that last sentence correctly. I believe it's the parent's job to lead with love and humility and often choosing to stay silent rather than defend or correct to get movement in the relationship. The word *estrangement* comes from a Latin word that means "to be treated as a stranger." For a parent or adult child to move from such an important relationship to being a stranger doesn't usually happen overnight, and it usually doesn't get fixed quickly. Too many parents want to spend their energy telling their adult child how wrong they are, trying to prove a point instead of pursuing peace. But this is the time not to blame or shame or make it about you but to instead do whatever it takes to keep the relationship moving in a good direction.

One well-meaning mom told me word for word what she said to her daughter: "I sacrificed my life for you. I gave you money. I did all I could to make you happy, and this is how you thank me, by not speaking to me or wanting a relationship with me?" She continued, "You have let me down time after time. You don't even have the courtesy to call me on my birthday or when I had knee surgery. And yet you tell me the problem is all me? How dare you talk to me like this, and how dare you treat me with such disrespect?" After she shared that, I gave her an unusually long pause and simply asked, "How did that work out for you?" With the same intensity she had used with her daughter, she replied, "She hasn't talked to me since, and she blocked my number." The little bubble in my head thought, "She may be right on some of her thinking about her daughter, but if she keeps communicating in this manner and with this intensity, she will only convince her daughter that being estranged is the right choice." No doubt her daughter could have done a better job of showing appreciation, and no doubt the mother could have found a kinder, gentler, and safer way to communicate with her daughter. Now their relationship is a mess, and with the daughter cutting her mother off and becoming estranged, the relationship just got more challenging and complicated. There are answers, but they don't come easily.

Parents Take the Lead

When parents share their stories about their adult child's estrangement, their emotions are understandably intense. Their responses are normally confusion mixed with anger, hurt, and even despair. They almost always are desperate for the relationship to change. The initial attempts to reconnect are usually misguided. One of the leading voices in this field, Tina Gilbertson, says it well: "It's not about who's right or wrong—it's about mending fences."[4] Parents have to take the lead to hold back, providing adult children the space and time to come back into the relationship. If we push too hard, we will drive them right out of our lives. I know that goes against the grain of what we want to say and do, but at first it's most effective to take baby steps and do a lot of listening.

Parents who are willing to take some responsibility for the breakdown and show some empathy will find that it goes a long way toward reconciliation and reconnecting. Many parents want to move directly to blame and shame, and that

---

4. Tina Gilbertson, *Reconnecting with Your Estranged Adult Child: Practical Tips and Tools to Heal Your Relationship* (New World Library, 2020), 125.

typically gets them nowhere. I once asked a woman who placed all the blame on her daughter if there was anything in her past she could apologize to her daughter about. She said, "She is the one who should be apologizing, not me." I said, "I get it, but showing empathy and apologizing for something will move your relationship along quicker than continuing to share your version of why you are estranged." She came back to me later and said, "I found something to apologize for from the past, so I apologized, and I sensed my daughter begin to open up toward me." This is why I encourage parents to take the lead. Use sentences like "I want to understand your perspective on how I have treated you." "I want to hear what you perceive my blind spots to be." Again, your job is not to tell your adult child how wrong they are and how right you are; rather, it is to get to the heart of the matter, and that comes through empathy. So choose empathy over confrontation. Focus on the process, not the outcome. Defensiveness, which is so natural, usually does little to no good in bringing back connection.

A mom and dad sat in my office sharing their estrangement story with a daughter who was in a lesbian relationship. They were angry at her, at her lover, and at the lover's parents for embracing this lifestyle. The father told me he finally reached out to his daughter, who said she was willing to meet with him. I asked how the meeting went.

He said, "I took her and her girlfriend to her favorite restaurant." (So far so good.) "Then after we ordered, I told her the reason I wanted to get together was because I needed to tell them what they were doing was an 'abomination.'" (Not a good first sentence to try and connect with your daughter.) I asked how they took being called an abomination. He said, "Well, my daughter started crying, and she and her girlfriend walked out of the restaurant." I gently asked, "What were you expecting from a conversation that started like that?" He said, "They needed to know how I felt and that what they were doing was wrong." He didn't answer my question, so I rephrased it. "I hear you, but what were you expecting or hoping would happen?" He came back with, "They need to stop this behavior immediately." Again, he didn't answer my question. I realized that he spoke to his daughter and her girlfriend before he ever took the time to think through how they would react to his comment. If you want to build trust and reopen dialogue, you may need to take things slowly, be thoughtful with your language, lead with love (as Jesus did), and practice kindness. That will move you toward reconciliation much quicker than dropping a word bomb to get their attention. The father's way of handling issues was not going to win his daughter back. When reconciling estrangement, we must learn quickly to agree to disagree without destroying the relationship.

This sounds counterintuitive, but when a relationship with your adult child has reached the estrangement level, it's rarely helpful to go on the offensive. It's a bit like when a person is drowning and the rescuer drowns because the drowning person pulls the rescuer down with them. A person in an estranged relationship often has a panic reaction spurred on by confrontation just like a drowning person becomes fearful and makes bad choices. Fear and panic in a relationship don't work well together. The wise parent doesn't escalate the situation but keeps the relationship in focus. This means bringing comfort and curiosity to the relationship. Be curious about your adult child's life, not defensive toward the situation. You can learn a lot when you are collecting information about feelings, responses, and actions. Tina Gilbertson says, "Take responsibility without accepting blame."[5] Again, it sounds counterintuitive, but one of the best and most powerful ways to bring connection back is to help your child feel seen, heard, and understood—even in the midst of conflict. Empathy brings connection.

Gilbertson has great insight here, "In order to recover a relationship with your child, you must find a way to put shame aside and invite compassion into your heart."[6] Compassion has a way of diffusing the emotions flying around the relationship. And yes, it's possible to validate your adult child's feelings without accepting blame.

The Impact of Estrangement

No matter the cause of the estrangement, there is a profound impact on you as a parent—and on your child. Never underestimate the emotional stress or loss or isolation brought on by estrangement. Recognize the impact on your life, but at the same time, try to imagine the situation from your adult child's

---

5. Gilbertson, *Reconnecting*, 119.

6. Tina Gilbertson, "Episode 58: Reconnecting with Your Estranged Adult Children with Tina Gilbertson," interview by Jim Burns, *HomeWord with Jim Burns*, May 29, 2025, www.listennotes.com/podcasts/homeword-with-jim/episode-58-reconnecting-with-Mt2R_TKU7Zo.

perspective, because they may be experiencing many of the same emotions but keeping them hidden from you. Research shows that people who experience estrangement have higher rates of depression and anxiety.[7] Common consequences of estrangement are shame, anger, guilt, resentment, desperation, and grief. The sense of loss can be immense. That is a very heavy load for a person to carry not just when they are thinking about the estranged relationship but with all their relationships. This emotional burden often seeps into work, home life, and the person's physical, mental, spiritual, and emotional health.

I recall a mom who called in to our radio show at New Life Live. Dr. Sheri Denham Keffer and I were hosting that day. This mom had a complicated relationship with her adult son. He was the youngest of her children and had been the easiest of her children to raise. In his early twenties, he separated from the family, moved to another state, and cut off contact with the family (a form of estrangement). At just twenty-six, he died in his sleep from a health complication. At his memorial service, a friend of his whom the mom had never met shared with her that her son had been gay. This mother was grieving on several levels. Dr. Sheri responded with deep and sincere empathy—psychologist to mom, and mom to mom. She introduced a term to this woman that I had never heard: *complicated bereavement*. As Dr. Sheri helped this woman through her deep pain of grief, I realized that

7. Morin, "Mental Health Impact of Estrangement."

complicated bereavement is what many parents experience with their estranged adult children.

The term *bereavement* is often used when a loved one dies. It marks a period of mourning the loss. Estrangement is not just loss of relationship, it is the death of a dream. Complicated bereavement in estrangement is being in a constant state of intense grief and loss. And just as with a death, individuals must go through a grief process. There is a finality to death, but estrangement has no closure. That is why it is essential for parents to get the counseling and support they need to become as healthy as possible, regardless of what happens in the relationship with the adult child. Reconciliation may happen, but it is most often a rocky and tough hill to climb. Thus, one of the central themes of this book is to prioritize the care of your own soul. You will want to get as physically, mentally, emotionally, and spiritually healthy as you possibly can to face the challenges of reconciliation.

Strategies to Move Forward

Every parent-child estrangement is different. What works for one family may not work for another. Yet there are some very helpful strategies that can help you move forward.[8]

---

8. Although the words are my own, I am deeply indebted to Tina Gilbertson and Joshua Coleman for their excellent resources on estrangement. I have learned so much from both of their works, especially *Rules of Estrangement* by Joshua Coleman and *Reconnecting with Your Estranged Adult Child* by Tina Gilbertson.

Work on Yourself, and Don't Depend on Your Adult Child to Meet Your Needs

The most effective strategy for moving forward in your relationship with your adult child is for you to become as emotionally healthy as possible. Estrangement wounds and confuses parents and adult children. While it does take two parties to get into the mess, the healthiest person in the room almost always does better in the long haul. Experts widely agree that if parents don't accept some of the responsibility for the role they played, it is much harder to reconcile. If parents don't lead with love, it is much more difficult to build a bridge. Dr. Henry Cloud and Dr. John Townsend wisely said, "When parents pull away in hurt, disappointment, and passive rage, they are sending a message to their youngster: You're lovable when you behave. You aren't lovable when you misbehave. The child translates that message to something like this: When I'm good, I am loved. When I am bad, I am cut off."[9]

Sometimes with estrangement, parents are still looking for their adult children to meet their emotional needs. Parents need to look elsewhere and develop other areas of support or they will usually be deeply disappointed. Meeting their parents' emotional needs is not the duty of a child, especially in the context of estrangement.

---

9. Henry Cloud and John Townsend, *Boundaries: When to Say Yes, How to Say No to Take Control of Your Life*, updated and expanded (Zondervan, 2017), 108.

Embrace "I'm Sorry"

Whenever possible, offer a sincere apology. In most relationships, one of the most powerful ways to reconnect is to apologize. More often than not, parents have something very real and substantive to apologize for. Do the hard work of finding your child's point of pain and how you caused or contributed to that pain. But if you are unsure of what to apologize for, listen to what your adult child is saying about you and apologize for how he or she feels without agreeing. "I'm so sorry you feel that way, and if I have not shown you love in this disagreement, then I truly am sorry. I love you, and I want us to be connected."

Those words carry far more power than a conversation I had with a dad who was estranged from his daughter. He had a negative relationship with his daughter and what I call a "low contact" estrangement, which means he was not completely cut off from her. He had lived a life of being unfaithful to her mother, and the divorce had been painful and messy. His daughter sided with her mom in the divorce. She rarely would return calls or saw him—perhaps once a year at best. Once he told me about his part in the divorce, I thought I asked a simple question: "Have you ever considered apologizing to your daughter for your part in the divorce?" With anger in his eyes, he responded, "I have nothing to apologize for, and my daughter needs to respect me as her father!" I'm seldom speechless, but his response stumped me. My guess is that minus a heartfelt apology, he is never going to have a good relationship with his daughter.

Gary Chapman is a mentor in my life and has written some amazing books on marriage and family. In a book he cowrote with Jennifer Thomas, they outlined five ways to apologize.[10] Learning these can dramatically improve your ability to reconcile with others, as could have been the case with this father and daughter. Here they are:

1. *Expressing regret.* "I am so deeply sorry, and I did not want to hurt you with my words. Please forgive me."
2. *Accepting responsibility.* "I'm very sorry. I take full blame for unleashing my anger toward you. That was all about me and not about you. Please forgive me."
3. *Making restitution.* "I am so sorry. I know I offended your husband, and I'd like to make it right by meeting with him (and you) and offering an apology. Plus, I'd like to pay him for the work he did at our house. I never wanted to take advantage of him. Please forgive me."
4. *Genuinely expressing the desire to change your behavior.* "I'm very sorry. I can understand how you felt belittled by my teasing, and I will not do that again. In fact, I decided to see a counselor about my behavior because I know I caused you some emotional pain. Please forgive me."
5. *Requesting forgiveness.* "I am very sorry and recognize my part in our estrangement. I created a barrier to our relationship. Will you accept my heartfelt apology?"

---

10. These five phrases come from Gary Chapman and Jennifer Thomas, *The Five Apology Languages: The Secret to Healthy Relationships* (Northfield, 2022).

Few things are as powerful as a meaningful, heartfelt apology. And speaking of apologies, we must be willing to forgive our adult children's mistakes even when what they did feels totally disobedient or disrespectful. Our instruction on forgiveness comes from none other than Jesus. In a powerful conversation on forgiveness between Peter and Jesus, the disciple asked him, "Lord, how many times shall I forgive my brother or sister who sins against me?" Peter, thinking this was quite generous, added, "Up to seven times?" Jesus answered, "I tell you, not seven times, but seventy-seven times" (Matt. 18:21–22). If you want a breakthrough in your relationship, begin with forgiveness. You can forgive and still have solid boundaries.

Embrace a Relationship with Different Values

With any adult who has strayed from family values, there will be differences of opinion and lifestyle. As mentioned in previous chapters, it's our job as parents to *agree to disagree*. You can disagree on many subjects but still have a respectful and loving relationship. Significant differences in values are the cause of many estranged relationships. It takes work and discipline to embrace a loving relationship over lifestyle choices or hurt feelings. At the Burns family Thanksgiving dinner, we have a "no politics spoken here policy." We have some passionate people on both sides of the political spectrum in our family, and we have found it's better to focus on what unites us rather than what divides us at a family dinner.

A friend of mine who comes from a conservative theological background asked his son out to lunch. His son was considering a gender identity change. Over lunch he said, "Son, the first thing I want to say is I love you no matter what. You know how your mom and I feel and what we think about your behavior. However, I want you to know we love you. Period. We will need to agree to disagree. I know that will be difficult for both of us, but I love you, son." I respect my friend. He led with love; he acknowledged the differences in beliefs and morals. He admitted it would be difficult and ended with love. Too often when there are strong differences in values, conversations spiral into anger and defensiveness—from both sides. It's easy to go there. But a parent should never mirror their adult child's anger with anger, or their adult child's hurt with hurt. Don't exchange accusations—that only escalates the situation. Instead, be the one who leads with calm, love, and grace.

Write a Letter or Email

Experts in the field of estrangement agree that one of the most powerful and helpful tools in moving toward reconciliation is writing a letter or an email. For whatever reason, when estranged parents and their child meet up, things can go south quickly. A short, loving, clear, and respectful letter acknowledging the estrangement can move the relationship closer toward reconciliation. However, you have to be careful how you write the letter. Here are some dos and don'ts:

Do

- Acknowledge the estrangement.
- Lead with love.
- Be kind.
- Be clear that you hope for reconciliation.
- Be respectful.
- Keep it short.

Don't

- Don't bring up the issues in the letter.
- Don't be defensive.
- Don't get lost in the weeds of the relationship.
- Don't vent your frustration.
- Don't tell them why they are wrong, and you are right.
- Don't blame.

The goal of a letter or email is to reestablish the connection and change the tone of the relationship from tension to tenderness. Here is an example:

> Hi Dena,
>
> I know we have been through a difficult patch in our relationship. [acknowledgment] You are always close to my heart, and I want you to know I love you deeply and always will. [love] I heard from your sister that you moved, and I bet your new place looks amazing. You have always been so gifted at creating a beautiful environment to live in. [kindness] I'd love to see it someday if and when that feels right

for you, but I also want to be respectful of your time and feelings. [clear and respectful]

I know that your favorite meal is Italian, so I've enclosed a gift card to a great Italian restaurant in your area. I love you, and when you are ready, I'd love to get a coffee with you.

Love,

Mom

Take the Time to Heal

Reconciling an estranged relationship usually takes time. Immediate breakthroughs can happen, but that is not the norm. Allowing your adult child to heal may take space and time. That means you will need an extra dose of patience. Remember: You are in it for the long haul. While the healing process is taking place, respect their limits and don't force a quick reconciliation.

As you move toward the healing stage, you may want to consider having a counselor help you develop a game plan. There is nothing like a discerning counselor to give insight and wisdom. There are also a few excellent books and blogs available that offer encouragement and direction for estranged parents. It's hard to move through the reconciliation process on your own. If you can find a counselor or author who can help you move forward, it is worth the time and effort.[11]

While this chapter touches on key principles, there's much

11. My three favorite counselor resources for estrangement with adult children are Kathy Cunningham (aseedofhopecc.com), Tina Gilbertson (tinagilbertson.com), and Joshua Coleman (drjoshuacoleman.com). Check out their resources as well as counseling options.

more available through the experts—and especially through one-on-one counseling. Even if things are not going well today, stay in the story the best you can. I know a couple who had been estranged from their adult child for twelve years—by the child's choice, not theirs. They would be the first to admit they didn't always get everything right. However, sometime in the first year of the estrangement, they taped a promise from the Bible to their bathroom mirror. It read: "[Be] confident of this, that he who began a good work in you will carry it on to completion until the day of Christ Jesus" (Phil. 1:6). They believed that at birth their child had been a gift from God. Furthermore, although they had been in a tough place with that child, with perseverance and patience they prayed that what God had started as good would one day end up as good again. That is exactly what happened. Their child wandered, caught up in confusing choices and a difficult season of life. But one day they got the call they had been praying and hoping for. Their child wanted to come home for a visit. Today they are reconciled, reconnected, and moving forward.

CHAPTER 8

WHEN YOUR RELATIONSHIP IS TOXIC AND COMPLICATED

Sometimes toxicity in a family sneaks in slowly and takes you by surprise. You ask, "How did we get to this point?" Other times and more commonly, it's been a part of the family dynamic for a long time, sometimes even generational.

Craig and Melinda are working hard to be the transitional generation and not follow in the footsteps of their parents and grandparents and even great-grandparents when it comes to having a toxic and dysfunctional family. They would be the first to say it hasn't been easy. They have had to fight the battle of coming from a toxic family environment. In Craig's family, there is a long line of alcoholism, violence, and likely untreated mental illness. Melinda told me there were no stable marriages on either side of her family tree. When Craig and Melinda got married, neither had any idea what a loving and connected family looked like. But here is the good news: They eventually identified the family history of toxicity and dysfunction and decided to change the trajectory of their family. And it worked. Today they not only have a quality marriage but have moved the needle from toxic family history to healthy and stable family. It took a deep desire to break the chains of dysfunction, and they worked hard at it. No one said it would be easy, but Craig and Melinda—and countless other families—are turning the page on toxic and complicated negative family patterns. What about you?

At its basic core, a toxic family is marked by consistent patterns of harmful behaviors toward one another, constant destructive interactions. These behaviors can include emotional, physical, or spiritual misconduct. Oddly, many toxic families have really good connection. One dad, in the midst of some major toxic behavior with his adult children, said to me, "One minute I'm thinking I'm crazy and they're normal, and the next minute I'm thinking they're crazy and I'm normal." He added, "Then there are those times where we seem to actually be doing quite well as a family. That is, until the next phone call that goes sideways or the vicious argument between the siblings or somebody drinks too much." Yes, there are families that come from a long line of healthy interaction, multigenerational vacations, and a legacy of solid living. But in general, there's a lot of brokenness in families, and that messiness often shapes our relationships more than we realize.

Signs of a Toxic Family Environment

What does a toxic family look like? Actually, it looks like your neighbors, your friends at church, and possibly your family. Following are seven signs of a toxic family.[1]

1. *They have no regard for boundaries and give you no breathing room.* It's parents of adult children who are still

1. This is in no way meant to be an all-inclusive chapter on the toxic family but rather is a big-picture view. If you believe you do have a toxic family, I recommend you talk with a trained counselor who can help you work through your issues.

giving unsolicited advice. It's making your business their business. It's the mother who would just walk unannounced into the home of her son and daughter-in-law at 6:30 in the morning. Or an adult child who is so enmeshed in the relationship that they are constantly telling their parents how to live and manage life. Someone once said, "Good fences make good neighbors." The same is true for families. Boundaries should cause safety, not chaos. When boundaries are ignored, family members tend to use fear, obligation, and guilt to try to get what they want. They ignore requests like "Don't call me at work unless it's an emergency." Enmeshed kids believe their parents are still extensions of themselves, and vice versa. One of the key issues in a toxic relationship is what is commonly called "mother enmeshment." This is when the mom can't let go of her adult child. She continues to enable dependency. If you describe your family as toxic, you may want to go back and review chapter 5 on boundaries.

2. *They regularly ghost you.* Ghosting can be very toxic in a family. It's a relatively new term that means a loved one is ignoring you. Parents of adult children complain constantly that they don't get phone calls or texts returned. They feel cut out of the relationship. Ghosting can be intermittent or constant. If your attempts to connect go unanswered, then you are probably being ghosted. Or if your child regularly bails out on established plans or fails to make or keep commitments, they could be

ghosting you. Other times it's not ghosting, and we might be just a bit too sensitive. We always need to look at their intent, whether they are just busy or not as connected as you would like. It's important to discern whether you're dealing with ghosting or just a difference in communication styles.

3. *They regularly gaslight you.* The term *gaslighting* comes from the 1938 play and 1944 movie *Gaslight*. It's the story of a manipulative husband who convinces his wife she is going insane. If there is gaslighting going on in your home, it could be constant criticism and judgment that can be manipulative. People who gaslight you minimize your feelings while avoiding taking responsibility for their own actions. They lie to make themselves look good and cause you to doubt yourself. Any home filled with constant criticism, judgment, and manipulation is toxic and emotionally unsafe.
4. *They make the "blame game" an Olympic sport.* In some families, the blame game becomes a way of life. When a lot of blaming is going on, someone is probably playing the role of victim. Psychologist Jeffrey Bernstein wrote, "Don't compromise your worth by riding on a horse named Victim and repeatedly heading to the same rodeo." Blame will cause distrust and division, not resolution.
5. *They disrespect different beliefs and feel judged or shamed.* This happens when parents fail to show their adult child grace while they are still in the process of

figuring out their identity or are violating family values. This doesn't mean we can't bring up a concern, but we need to do it in love or they will think our love is conditional and limited. Parents may not intend to withhold love, but if love feels conditional, that damages trust. As Rachel Wolchin says, "Maturing is realizing how many things don't require your comment." Again, it's possible to show unconditional love while not approving of behaviors.

6. *The parents are not practicing self-awareness.* Lynn was not very self-aware. She was a nice enough person and a very engaged mother to her kids. But she was what some people have called "high maintenance of the worst kind—she thinks she's low maintenance." I always smile when I hear that phrase, but there is some truth to that statement for all the parents who are simply not self-aware and don't think they are part of the problem. Many adult children tell me that their parents are clueless when it comes to their part in the broken relationship. After meeting with hundreds of parents, I think the adult children are often right. We have both an internal self-awareness and external self-awareness, and both are important. Internal is based on how much we know ourselves, and external is based on how well we understand how others view us. A parent lacking self-awareness and who is not willing to look honestly at their own blind spots or hear from their community is going to remain in toxic relationships.

7. *They try to make changes with family members who are still holding on to active addictions.* The principle always holds true: People with addictions are emotionally unavailable. Until people choose recovery over their addiction, things will remain toxic. Addiction is so powerful that we often can't work in the other issues of a relationship until the addiction is addressed. Kelli was a thirtysomething mom with three kids. When she was sober, she was a good mom, a good wife, and an okay daughter. But the problem was, she was rarely sober. Her husband had tried everything to get her to stop drinking. She would say she would quit, but when her addiction took over, she lied, compromised, and did whatever she could do to fuel her addiction. Even her kids begged her to quit drinking. They had been embarrassed numerous times. The toxicity level in the family and extended family was very high. One day after school, with her three kids in the back of her SUV, she wrapped the vehicle around a tree. It frightened her. She was fortunate it was a tree and not a pedestrian or another driver. With the help of a supportive but fed-up husband, she entered a treatment center. A month later she came out sober and happy with a plan to remain free of her addiction for the rest of her life. She knows it's a "live one day at a time" life commitment. She keeps working her plan, and the family dynamics keep improving. What is needed in millions of toxic homes are courage and humbling

> honesty on the part of the addict and the parents. I've met hundreds of toxic addicts with regrets. I have never met a person who regretted choosing sobriety. Given that fact, the real change comes once they are beginning the recovery process and are sober. The healing process just doesn't work when their addictions are active.

The seven signs we covered earlier are just a starting point. How many of these toxic family patterns do you recognize in your family?

- emotional and physical abuse
- lack of trust, freeloading
- never "good enough"
- contempt
- unreal expectations
- controlling
- guilting
- unpredictable
- escalated anger

I'm sure you can add your own words and phrases to this list. Here is the fact: You are not responsible for anyone else's happiness—not your spouse's, not your kids', not your mother's, not your boss's. You can't find true contentment for your adult children. What they most need from you is for you to be the best version of you. The surest way to make ourselves miserable is to get involved with everyone else's business. You can't want their health more than they want their health. You can't please someone with a toxic personality and toxic life. As the saying goes, "If you try to please everyone, you will please no one." I've learned that people will hear words, but they feel your attitude. The greatest thing we can do for our adult children, our spouse, and others is to do everything we can to get as healthy as possible.

There is a powerful story in the Bible of Jesus approaching a man who had been lame for thirty-eight years (John 5:1–15). They met at a pool in Jerusalem called Bethesda. People with all kinds of infirmities would spend each day around the pool because an angel of the Lord would periodically stir up the water and the first person in the pool would be healed. Jesus went straight up to this man, who had been infirm for thirty-eight years and asked a very important question: "Do you want to get well?" You would think the man would enthusiastically say, "Yes!" But instead, he made an excuse, "I have no one to help me into the pool when the water is stirred. While I am trying to get in, someone else goes down ahead of me." Jesus didn't accept the excuse, but simply said, "Get up. Pick up your mat and walk." And the man was cured that very day. The question Jesus asked was, "Do you want to get well?" That is the same question he asks all of us. The man had to obey and pick up his mat in faith. For many in a toxic family, their "mat" is a decision to seek help and do the work it takes to get well. In Luke 5:12–13, we see Jesus' heart when another man who had leprosy said to him, "Lord, if you are willing, you can make me clean." These three words came out of Jesus' mouth: "I am willing." And he is willing to do what it takes for your family to heal.

Healing a Toxic Family

What will it take to heal a toxic family?

Of course there are no easy answers. We all miss the mark, and one person in the family, like yourself, may choose to move toward healing while another isn't ready or doesn't want it. But that shouldn't stop you from going for it. Regardless of the immediate outcome for everyone, it's always the best decision to pursue health for yourself.

Keep in mind that if your desire is to move toward a more connected relationship with your adult child, your desire for intimacy may be more than they can give. Healing and healthy relationships take time. Patience may be your greatest asset in this process. Here are three important decisions you can make for yourself.

1. Seek a Healthy Marriage

This may surprise you, but a healthy marriage may become your greatest benefit and blessing. When a married couple has built a strong marriage, they can face the toxicity of a family together. They can support and lean on each other. I know it's not easy, and often it's complicated. I recently received an email from a brand-new empty-nest mom who had listened to my podcast. She wrote, "The biggest problem in our marriage relationship is our extremely different ways of dealing with our adult children and their problems. If we don't get help, we are not going to make it in our marriage!" I get it. One of the most frequent sources of conflict between Cathy and me has been our approaches to parenting. In fact, more couples are divorcing after age fifty than ever before.[2] I believe that one of the more silent reasons for the graying of divorce is the emotional toll that comes from navigating deep disagreements about how to respond when adult children are violating our values and straying from our faith.

The couples I see who are intentional about nurturing a healthy marriage tend to do better in life. I have the privilege to speak at a marriage conference a few times each year at Chick-fil-A's WinShape Retreat Center in Mt. Berry, Georgia. My topic is "Empty Nest Success for Your Marriage." Do you know what the retreat couples say is the number one issue they have in their marriages? It's navigating life with their adult children. It beats out communication, sexual intimacy, and all the other topics.

So if you are struggling with your adult kids in your marriage, you are not alone. Maybe it's time for a reset. Maybe it's time to have some serious fun together. Your marriage is more than your shared role as parents—it's a relationship worth prioritizing. Most marriages don't end because of abuse, adultery, or addictions; they just drift apart. Can you fall out of love? I believe you can. But you can also light the spark again. My friend Arlene Pellicane said this about marriage on my

2. Charlotte Huff, "More Couples Are Divorcing After Age Fifty Than Ever Before," *Monitor on Psychology* 54, no. 8 (November 1, 2023): www.apa.org/monitor/2023/11/navigating-late-in-life-divorce.

podcast: "You don't stumble upon a marriage filled with treasures, you *build* such a life and marriage."

And if you are single, then seeking a healthy relationship with your singleness is just as important for you. My experience with single parents is that they are often too busy or too distracted to celebrate a job well done. Single parents are often some of the bravest and most courageous parents I know. Many single parents with adult children who are straying play the blame game on their own life experiences. This is a time to practice large doses of self-care and support from other parents. Don't think you can work through the issues with your adult children alone. Find trusted, safe relationships that can help you navigate this season of your life.

2. Set Healthy Boundaries and Take the High Road

Yes, toxic family relationships are complicated. As we explored in chapter 5, setting healthy boundaries will foster a good relationship. That's the answer to developing a better relationship. When you set boundaries, you are assertively taking the high road. You are choosing not to manipulate or be manipulated. You will love your adult child but not be their punching bag or turn them into a punching bag. You will love yourself in a healthy way by not being abusive and not allowing abusive talk toward you. Taking the high road means not beating yourself up for your past mistakes but bringing God into the picture. His grace for you brings peace, and when you have peace, you will be equipped to make wiser decisions with those who don't have peace.

My dad was an alcoholic. Although some of my friends in the field of counseling don't like the term "functioning alcoholic," he was the closest thing to it. No, he didn't do emotional closeness all that well, but he was still one of the most influential people in my life. He showed up at every Little League game and at my high school sports. I count myself very fortunate. At the same time, as I got older his drinking increased and a friend of mine told me I may need to lower my expectations for a deeper connection with Dad. He was right. I'm an eternal optimist and just kept hoping I would have a closer relationship with him, but while he was drinking, he was incapable of giving that to me. So I set up some boundaries, continued to love him, and lowered my expectations. This went on for many years. Everything wasn't horrible, but as a dad myself, I knew I was giving my daughters much more than my dad could give to me.

One day Dad had too much to drink, and he almost put his motorhome over a cliff with my mom in the vehicle. After seeing photos of the RV hanging over that cliff, all of us were aware that my dad and mom were blessed to be alive. That experience scared my dad. I visited him the next day and had an intervention for him to go to an alcoholic treatment center at the age of sixty-eight. He did, and he was the oldest guy there by more than thirty years. Before Dad left the rehab center, he decided to enter a life of sobriety. He stuck with it. When he died twenty-one years later, I was aware of how blessed I was to have had twenty-one years of his sobriety in my life. He had become a new man, and we had grown closer. I was fortunate because I had lowered my expectations yet had received more than I ever imagined. Sometimes we must set the right boundaries to be surprised by joy.

3. Seek Help, Support, and Wisdom

I talked with a couple after one of my Doing Life with Your Adult Children seminars. The relationship with their two adult children was complicated and intense. The woman told me she was experiencing anxiety and depression and having a difficult time coping with her life, her marriage, and her work, along with physical symptoms like headaches and insomnia. After listening to their story about the toxicity of their relationship with their adult children and her emotional and physical ailments, I asked a simple question. "Have you ever sought help for all that is going on in your life?" The wife's answer surprised me: "I don't think there is anyone who could help or understand." Her husband said, "She is a bit emotionally paralyzed from everything." And I'm sure he was right.

My response went something like this: "If you were walking down the street in your city and someone came up to you and hit you with a two-by-four, my guess is someone would assess the situation and get you immediate medical attention." She nodded. "I perceive that your trauma is on the inside. People around you can't see it, but the damage is just as bad or worse. It has taken a toll on your health, your mind, and your emotions, and it is impacting all areas of your life. Experts in trauma may help you with your many complicated issues."

Her husband wanted to get help for her, but she seemed

hesitant, only semi-willing to seek help. I referred her to a trauma therapist I knew and trusted. This woman (and couple) was going to need a mindset shift and the counsel, support, and wisdom of others to have a breakthrough in her life.

Counseling, therapy, coaching, talking with a wise friend, and sitting down with your pastor are all good ideas. This woman needed more intense therapy. She needed support from friends and time with her pastor for spiritual care, but her situation needed a licensed, trained therapist who could help unravel the complicated problems with her adult children and some of her other issues. A professional counselor would possess the skills to help her feel more comfortable in talking through her issues to find peace. A counselor could also assess if some of the complications in the relationship with her adult children might have been caused by addictive behaviors or mental illness or some form of abuse from the past. A counselor doesn't do all the work for the client and tell the client what to do. A good counselor helps to diagnose the situation and looks at ways to resolve the problems.

A toxic or dysfunctional family dynamic is different from normal family struggles. The feelings are tense, unstable, and charged with emotion. That is when we need an expert to help us. Some people say, "I can't afford therapy." That is not an excuse. Free counseling or low-cost counseling on a sliding scale is available, as well as medical care. Some people say their church doesn't believe in counseling. Okay, but that might be just a certain type of counseling. So go with what feels right for you. Seek help. A battle for your mind, relationships, and heart is taking place, and the Bible speaks clearly about gaining wisdom for battles: "Where there is no counsel, the people fall; but in the multitude of counselors there is safety" (Prov. 11:14 NKJV).

Just as there are many reasons we go to a medical doctor, there are many good reasons to seek counsel and wisdom from a trained counselor. Here are just a few:

- To manage stress and anxiety
- For support and insight in life transitions and life complications (including dealing with an adult child issue)
- To improve primary relationships
- For personal growth and self-discovery
- To help get emotions under control
- To help with an addiction (alcohol, drugs, sex, gambling, to name a few)
- To deal with a loss
- To resolve problems in your marriage or with a family member
- To find help for trauma, including PTSD
- To understand identity issues, whether in general or sexual
- To learn how to resolve conflicts
- To manage grief

Everyone can benefit from a counselor to provide wisdom, insight, and support.

One day over breakfast, I was sitting with my friend Dr. Henry Cloud on his boat, eating a breakfast burrito and catching up on life. Henry is one of America's most insightful counselors, a prolific writer and thinker. I asked him, "As a counselor, how do you view your work with people?" I thought his answer was profound. He said, "I don't just view myself as a counselor. I disciple people to be more of what God created them to be." I remember thinking that morning that that's the kind of people I want around me. Seek out people who have a similar philosophy of life and mission as Henry. Those people are in your community; you just have to search for them. If you are willing to do the hard work of walking through your life circumstances with a counselor, then do the hard work it takes to find a good counselor.

If you identify your family as toxic, you already know life is complicated and there are no easy answers. But it is very possible to bring your life and family to a better place regardless of your circumstances or others' choices. Your job is to get as healthy as you possibly can. It's going to take building the right support systems around you and leaning on God's strength. The ride may be bumpy, but hopefully the bumps will smooth out a bit, and as you look back you will see how far you've come. In the movie *We Bought a Zoo*, Benjamin Mee, played by Matt Damon, says, "You know, sometimes all you need is twenty seconds of insane courage. Literally twenty seconds of just embarrassing bravery. And I promise you, something great will come of it."[3] What decisions do you need to make to move away from toxicity to health?

Common Causes of Toxicity with Your Adult Children

The following is not an exhaustive list of causes of toxicity with adult children, and this book is not meant to provide all the answers. I recommend that you seek qualified counseling help with these issues from experts in the field. They understand the patterns and the pathology of these issues.

- abuse
- abusive spouse or girlfriend or boyfriend
- anxiety disorders
- bipolar
- can't hold a job
- can't or won't leave
- child wants (or needs) money
- chronically depressed
- crime
- criminal behavior
- damage to home

3. *We Bought a Zoo*, screenplay by Aline Brosh McKenna and Cameron Crowe, based on the book of the same name by Benjamin Mee, directed by Cameron Crowe (20th Century Fox, 2011).

- eating disorder
- failure in school or work
- gender identity issues
- major dysfunctional relationship with opposite sex
- mental illness
- money issues
- out of control behavior
- parent has unfair expectations
- physical threats
- suicidal
- violent
- weapons

Don't try to manage these issues on your own. Seek trained professional help.

CHAPTER 9

BREAKING DOWN WALLS AND BUILDING BRIDGES

Many of the conversations I have with parents of adult children who have strayed could be summed up with this phrase: "Life was good . . . and then it wasn't." The story often begins with a child who was kind, responsible, and even thriving through the teen years, only to choose a different direction in their young adulthood, far from what the parents had hoped, dreamed, or prayed. Each story has its own set of twists and turns. But too often, because nobody ever went to "adult child parenting school," and most of us never learned how to communicate effectively, we get stuck in a cycle of tension and disappointment. Emotional walls go up on both sides, and most of us don't know how to break down those walls because both the parents and the adult child think that if the other would change their behavior, life would be good again. It's rarely that simple.

Growing up, I wouldn't have said my family excelled in communication. It never occurred to me that anything was lacking—it was just how we interacted, and I had no frame of reference to know any different. Once I left home, went to college, got married, and eventually became a parent, I brought many of my poor communication patterns with me. This was my "normal." I have no doubt some of those communication habits that I had imitated from my family also played a strong role in all my relationships, from friends to work associates.

Then came a moment I'll never forget. I know exactly where I was sitting: in the lunchroom at eHarmony in West Los Angeles, having lunch with one of my mentors, Neil Clark Warren, the founder of eHarmony. Neil is older, wiser, and much more brilliant than me. Our mutual passion as Christian leaders is to help relationships thrive. As I shared with him my frustration about how I often defaulted to communication habits I had picked up from my family, he looked at me like a coach and mentor and said, "Jim, communication is a learned trait." I then realized that I could learn better communication tools, new ways of connecting, to enhance all my relationships. For those of us with adult children, especially when we're not on the same page about life or values, learning new approaches to communication is critical. We need to build bridges, not walls.

Building Walls: The Good, the Bad, and the Ugly

When it comes to communication, especially with our adult children, we all build walls. Some walls in relationships can be healthy. Walls can be a boundary, and boundaries can keep relationships healthy. Boundaries bring protection and security. Yes, some walls keep us safe. Healthy walls can be a good thing—something that guards our hearts and preserves the integrity of relationships.

Years ago I was speaking in Beijing, China, with my daughter Rebecca, and we took a trip to the Great Wall of China. Wow! What a magnificent structure. It stretches 13,170 miles from east to west and is one of the great wonders of the world. When I asked our tour guide why China built such a wall, he explained that it was built to protect China from its enemies. Yes, some walls or boundaries in our life protect us. We build walls or boundaries in our life to guard ourselves from hurt, betrayal, fear, and temptation. I have placed boundaries in my own life to protect my marriage, guard against addiction, and help me make healthy choices. Building a wall can serve a very real purpose for good. The fence in our back yard keeps the neighbor's dog from invading our back yard. That's a good thing.

Walls can also separate and isolate. They lead to power struggles, emotional pain, loneliness, and distance. Often walls erode the fun and joy we used to share, replacing them with fighting, boredom, or even breakdown in connection, resulting in our adult child feeling unloved. Author Jim Rohn once said, "The walls we build around us keep sadness out but also keep out the joy." Walls in a relationship can block intimacy and connection. Have you built walls in your relationship with your adult child? It's likely if they have strayed that you have built up some walls and so have they.

Before we look at how to create healthy bridges, let's look at some of the walls we build—consciously or not.

Building Walls (Negative Conflict Patterns)

Tension

Walls in a relationship usually start with some type of tension. Tension is often a natural part of the transition from parenting a child to relating to an adult. It can show up in many ways: friction, problems, pain, misunderstanding, frustration, broken boundaries, violated values, deconstruction of faith.

Instead of leaning into healthy conflict resolution, we often default toward old, negative patterns. Most of us gravitate toward our wall of choice when we feel hurt, confused, or threatened. As you read the following, consider which ones may apply to you—or your adult child.

THE WALL OF DEFENSIVENESS

Walls are a defense mechanism that hurt relationships. The wall of defensiveness is one of the most common and damaging because it blocks healthy communication and connection. Many of us don't even realize we are being defensive. We're quick to spot it in our adult child, but it's much harder to recognize it in ourselves. Being defensive is a natural way to handle conflict, but it's not healthy. It's poor communication.

Your son or daughter does something that you don't think is a good idea. You confront them. They respond with a defensive comment. You say something like, "You are being so defensive. I'm just trying to point out your problem." They respond, "What? Me, defensive? It's not me. You are the one who is being defensive!" Now the conversation has shifted from the subject matter to who is being the most defensive. If you or your adult child is defensive, a wall is quickly built even higher. Since defensiveness is a form of self-protection, if your adult child is being defensive, it's because they perceive you as a threat. Unfortunately, defensive behavior creates a reciprocal cycle.

Defensive communication means that someone is avoiding responsibility for their feelings, behavior, or consequences. It causes distance and shuts down healthy communication. When someone is defensive, they try to control the narrative and the conversation turns into blaming, shaming, attacking, and control. There is a lot of "you" and "I" language. Walls of defense go up and divide, while healthy communication shuts down.

THE WALL OF AVOIDANCE

This is a wall I know well. One of Cathy's lines to me early in our marriage was "Are you going to crawl into your cave again?" I don't like conflict. I avoid it at all costs. Avoidance is the silent killer of connection. A conflict avoider is one who withdraws from the fight instead of facing it and working through the conflict. People often fall into one of three categories: fight, flight, or freeze. The wall of avoidance leads by taking flight or withdrawing. There are other walls that lead with fighting and freezing. Those who flee actually think it's better not to fight through the issue, but that's wrong.

As we will see, there is a healthy way to confront an issue that brings connection and understanding. Withdrawal and avoidance create distance in the relationship that sometimes looks like pouting. At times an adult child will avoid and withdraw because they don't have the energy to communicate in an adult manner with their parents. I hear phrases like "My mom isn't going to listen anyway. She just wants to lecture, not hear me." These young adults are avoiding, but we may also need to ask ourselves if we have created a safe place for conversation.

THE WALL OF DETACHMENT

A very close cousin to the wall of avoidance is the wall of detachment or isolation. Some would describe this as the freeze category. Instead of expressing our thoughts or feelings, we shut down. We stuff and repress our feelings, keeping them all inside. Author John Powell said it this way: "When I repress my emotions, my stomach keeps score." What we don't deal with emotionally tends to come out in physical, mental, or relational ways. Many people don't realize what they are feeling because they didn't grow up in an environment where emotions were allowed to be expressed. The problem with detachment is that it can appear or be interpreted like we don't care, or our adult child doesn't care, but nothing could be farther from the truth. If we isolate and detach, emotional needs leak out and tend to get redirected into distractions, escapes, bitterness, and resentment. Detachment doesn't solve the problem, it just delays the healing.

THE WALL OF DENIAL

Denial is when we fail to take responsibility for our part in the conflict. "This conflict is 100 percent about him and not about me." I get nervous when someone tells me, "I did nothing wrong!" Really? Relationships are always a two-way street. Don't allow yourself to build a wall of denial, which will only keep everyone from healing.

THE WALL OF FANTASIA

Adult children may fantasize about what life would be like without their parents' involvement and with all their own freedom. The wall of fantasia can be a subtle wall a person builds around themselves if life gets too difficult or hectic to handle. It comes in the form of anything we use as an escape from the reality of life. It might be working too much, spending too much, eating too much, binge-watching Netflix, or spending hours on social media. Many people fail to deal with their issues and make poor choices with the idea that the grass is greener outside of any family relationship.

THE WALL OF PASSIVE-AGGRESSIVE BEHAVIOR

Passive-aggressive behavior comes from the inability or unwillingness to say what you mean in a respectful way. This wall is sneaky and destructive. When parents or adult children get their feelings hurt, they sometimes shut down any progress being made. Some people are wired to be passive (not saying anything) or aggressive (disrespectful). Passive-aggressive communication means that instead of using positive, direct words to communicate needs, the person defaults to indirect, unhealthy, and negative behaviors.

For example, your adult child doesn't fully come clean on an issue. Instead of directly telling you they won't be staying home for all of Thanksgiving Day, they don't mention they are leaving right after dinner to be with their friends. They simply leave, and it comes across as rude, withdrawing from family and being distant. A passive-aggressive response might be saying you aren't upset but going around the house slamming doors, acting irritably, and withdrawing as a form of punishment. Passive-aggressive behavior is about words that don't match actions. It's the adult child or parent who screams, "There is nothing wrong!" The words say one thing, but the actions say something very different.

One mom told me that when her son moved back in the house, he spent most of his time watching TV and wasn't pitching in to help around the house. One night she asked him if he would go to the store for her. He declined, saying he was busy doing something else. The mom went to the store, but before she left, she put the TV remote in her purse instead of saying anything about him watching TV. When she came home, he was sitting on the couch watching a show. She said, "How did you turn it on?" He looked up and said, "I have another remote in my room." Her passive-aggressive behavior backfired.

THE WALL OF ANGER

It seems like there is a lot of anger going around when an adult child strays: anger at the child, anger at the parents, anger at our spouse, and anger at ourselves. Angry people often like to fight, but it is seldom in a healthy way. Here is something interesting about anger—it's rarely the first emotion we feel, it's a secondary emotion. That means if I am displaying anger, I need to ask myself, "Why do I have all this anger?" Could it be hurt, embarrassment, sadness, frustration, or fear, to name a few? Letting a wall of anger go unchecked can turn into rage that gets directed at our loved ones. Anger produces what is commonly called a "harsh startup" in communication—when conversations begin with blame, accusation, or elevated emotion. A harsh startup closes down healthy communication. It leads to people making hurtful comments in anger, and then those words cause wounds that are hard to forget and build walls that are even harder to break.

Anger is not all bad. But most people need to learn how to manage their anger. If it is not dealt with in a healthy way, anger and rage cause those harsh startups that end in conflict and disconnection.

The Result: Invalidation

When we build walls, the other person feels invalidated. They feel unseen, unheard, and unloved. They view the relationship as hopeless. Some give up trying. Walls signify that the builder can't see the good in the relationship. When people build walls, they become experts at pointing out the flaws in the other, but seldom the strengths. If you are negative all the time, not only will you build walls, but you will cause your child to build their own walls of defense. Make sure invalidation doesn't creep into the relationship.

Take a moment to reflect: What walls do you tend to build? This may be an oversimplification, but much of building a bridge to make a better relationship with your adult child will depend on how many and to what depth your walls are standing between you. Remember: Communication is a learned trait; you may not be able to change your adult child, but you can change you.

Breaking Down the Walls

Another famous wall—one that is no longer standing—is the Berlin Wall. That wall was very divisive. It was built to divide West Berlin from East Berlin. It kept families separated from one another. It kept a city, a country, and the world divided. The Berlin Wall represented a physical barrier that kept people detached and removed. It represented oppression and sadness for millions of people.

On June 12, 1987, President Ronald Reagan delivered the famous line "Mr. Gorbachev, tear down this wall!" A little over two years later, the wall came down and families were reunited. A divided world came together. Cathy and I were on a ministry trip to Eastern Europe on the other side of the wall on that famous day (November 9, 1989), and we witnessed firsthand people pouring out into the streets to sing, dance, and celebrate with joy that the wall had been torn down. The headline that day in a Romanian newspaper read, "And the Walls Came Tumbling Down."

When an adult child and parents begin the hard work of reconciliation as the walls are breaking down, just like with the Berlin Wall, there is reason to celebrate. It usually doesn't happen in one day. It's often a process, but what joy and hope it brings to all.

In the ancient world, cities were protected by walls that were difficult to climb, and there were no modern weapons, no cannons to knock them down. The most brilliant military strategists knew how to scale the walls, dig through, or even build bridges over them to get inside the city. In the Bible, King David, who was one of the greatest military strategists of his time, testified time and again that he would scale a wall. He had an unshakable confidence that God would strengthen him to conquer whatever walls stood before him. I have David's words from Psalm 18:29 on a note in my office: "With my God I can scale any wall" (NLT).

If your adult child has strayed, your options are either to move toward breaking down the barriers or to continue bumping up against those walls. Something called *reactive distancing* happens when parents continue to push, often with anxiety and pressure, and the adult child withdraws to protect their independence. You don't want that to happen, so you'll have to work at breaking down the walls you have built up between yourself and your adult child. This doesn't mean you start with your child, it means you start with you. As you break apart the wall—most likely by changing your communication strategy—you will do the delicate dance of tweaking your strategy, keeping in mind that you don't have to compromise your values. It can be done.

Even a small tweak to your strategy can make a difference. I once heard a pastor say in a sermon, "You will never change your life until you change something you do daily. The secret of success is found in your daily routine." He was talking about personal and spiritual disciplines, but the same is true with our kids. We often need to work on ourselves first. We must choose to release fear. I've heard it said, "Fear doesn't stop death, it stops life." We need to let go of the timeline we have in our mind for our adult child to change but not release the relationship.

How you respond to your adult child can either lessen the intensity of the situation or widen the gap. When you work at delicately breaking down the wall, you are aiming at their heart and not their actions, even if their actions are breaking your heart. Fostering understanding, empathy, and open communication is key. It involves looking beyond differences and disagreements to find common ground and shared experiences, which cultivates a deeper connection.

What You Can Do to Break Down the Walls

Don't miss the fact what when building bridges, we still must start with the same tension that caused the walls in the first place. But instead of going to a negative conflict pattern, we develop a positive pattern.

1. Treat Them with AWE

On my desk, I have a yellowed sticky note with the acronym AWE, which stands for affection, warmth, and encouragement. People respond to AWE. I want to be someone who offers AWE to all people on different levels. The kind of AWE that I give to my wife is different from the AWE I give a coworker or neighbor. What I have found with my adult children is that they respond to appropriate and authentic displays of affection, warmth, and encouragement. When you bring AWE to a relationship, you are improving emotional intimacy and connection. Emotional connection breaks down walls and builds connection. It's not always easy, especially if you didn't experience much emotional connection from your parents or even your spouse. Start by listening to your adult child—really listening. Listening is the language of love. James, the brother of Jesus, said it well: "Take note of this: Everyone should be quick to listen, slow to speak and slow to become angry" (James 1:19).

There is nothing like a good conversation with your adult child, but it may take holding thoughts, biting your tongue, and building emotional connection with listening and acceptance. We don't have to agree or compromise our beliefs to build a bridge of acceptance. God's unfailing love for us models this beautifully—his love and acceptance of us are not based on our actions, but on his relationship with us. Saint Francis of Assisi said it this way: "May I seek to understand rather than to be understood."

2. Healthy Connection

Words don't always lead to connection. Connection leads to words. I've noticed that with my wife, Cathy, and my adult children, emotional connection and understanding don't come from sitting at the kitchen table with a list of problems or "here's what's wrong with you" list. They come through shared experiences, fun, and enjoying one another's company. Yes, there are times when we need to talk or deal with conflict, but the best way to prepare is by building healthy emotional connection. Healthy connection is a bridge to better communication.

My friend Ron was having trouble with one of his adult sons floundering in life and making some poor choices. Ron had tried sitting at the table with his very long "what's wrong with you" list. The conversations weren't going anywhere. So Ron decided to take a road trip with his son. Together they planned a seven-day trip that included visiting beaches from Southern California to Northern California. They fished. They surfed. They biked. They ate a lot of good food and had other adventures.

Two things happened on that trip. First, they came back bonded as a dad and son. And second, the son became comfortable talking to his dad about some of his fears, concerns, and issues that had been holding him back from thriving. The deepest talks didn't happen at the beginning of the week; but toward the end of the week, something shifted inside his son and he started opening up and sharing. Sometimes Ron would say to his son, "Do you want my input or just my listening ear?" The difference was that now his son was inviting him to share his thoughts. His son said, "All of the stupidest things I have done involved drinking alcohol." Ron was able to bond with his son with total transparency, sharing he could say the same thing about himself when he was a young adult. Much of the advice Ron gave him had already been given at the kitchen table, but the connection made all the difference. Nonconfrontational connection opens up a closed spirit and reduces stress while building memories.

When you are connected with your adult children, you can become a "we" and begin to work together, with each person assuming responsibility to work through the conflict to find a meaningful resolution. Connection is the bridge to a renewed relationship. Deeper connection comes when dialogue and listening are initiated instead of one-sided communication. It grows when feelings are shared without placing blame. Connection comes when you seek common ground and learn to agree to disagree. Although it may not be easy, it is the best way to build a bridge.

3. Place Your Hope in God

God is not finished with your adult child's story. As we discussed in chapter 6 on deconstruction, it's not uncommon for adult children to drift away from the faith they were raised in. It can be shocking and painful, yes, but there is also some hope to be found. History tells us that God has never given up on his children. The Bible says it plainly: "God has said, 'Never will I leave you; never will I forsake you'" (Heb. 13:5). That is good news for you—and for your adult children, whether they realize it or not.

Some young adults have replaced Sunday worship with CrossFit, yoga, Pilates, or hikes. Some have replaced hearing the Word of God with brunch and coffee or sleeping in. Some have replaced the church with simply having family times with their kids. I'm a family guy and love the idea of family time, but I think it's possible to have good family time and connect with the one who created us in the first place. I'm in agreement with Viktor Frankl, the philosopher and Holocaust survivor who made this very insightful comment: "When a person can't find a deep sense of meaning, they distract themselves with pleasure." Pleasure seems to be a focus of many in this generation who have walked from their faith. Some adult kids got busy and distracted. For others it was a constant choice. They changed their morals, and that meant rejecting their faith. Still others left out of profound pain and suffering.

Here is some good news about our adult children and faith. Journalist Lauren Jackson reported in a fascinating *New York Times* article surprising and encouraging research about people of faith. She learned that there is overwhelming empirical support of the value of attending a house of worship, and adult children who have left their faith are beginning to recognize this. Jackson wrote, "People who practice religion tend to be happier than those who don't, a study by the Pew Research Center found."

If you are a parent of an adult child who has walked away from their faith, you can find hope in that things are shifting. Many young adults are searching to find something to believe in, and some of them say that they have missed the community they once had in church and are beginning to return. Data reveals that those who believe are "happier, healthier, and more fulfilled," and some in this generation of young adults are turning their hearts and minds back. That's all good news for people of faith.

You might be asking, "What does this have to do with breaking down the walls?" Everything.

Here is what you can do even if your children aren't in a place for dialogue yet: "Devote yourselves to prayer, being watchful and thankful" (Col. 4:2). This is great advice from the apostle Paul. Commit to pray daily for your adult children. Prayer connects you with the Comforter and with the Creator who cares even more deeply for your adult child than you do. Be watchful. Keep your eyes open to see how God is moving in their life. He does move, and he will. I wish I could guarantee you that your child will respond in the manner you hope for, but I can't. Watch for openings to connect your faith with theirs, but don't be preachy. Make it natural. Being watchful also will help you be aware of God's hand in their life. He may bring them a new Christian friend at work, or they may allow you to bring the grandkids to church. God will move, and when you see that happening, it will bring you hope. Watch for a week, a month, a year, a lifetime. And be thankful. A major part of prayer is giving thanks to God. Find everything you can possibly do to keep an attitude of gratefulness and thanksgiving. Do it because it's the right thing to do and because it will always give you the best perspective in your times of worry and doubt.

As you build bridges with your adult children, you will see change. Sure, you have to do the work to break down the walls, but it's worth it. A sign in my office reads, "Every child needs at least one person who is irrationally positive about them." That's your role—to be that person even if they aren't showing signs of change. And you will need to walk the fine line of love without enabling them or compromising your beliefs and boundaries. But in doing so, you will build bridges, not walls, and you will move from control to a genuine adult-to-adult relationship which you might get to enjoy more than you ever dreamed.

THANK YOU

I seldom think of myself as a writer. Maybe I should reconsider since I seem to write a book almost every year. Still, I write only when something stirs deeply within me. It's never been about the "business of writing"; it's always been about passion and purpose. This book didn't just emerge from passion; it was born of a strong burden. Over the past few years, I've listened to thousands of parents of adult children who have experienced pain, shame, hurt, and confusion over an adult child who has strayed.

I'm grateful to the many people who have walked alongside me through this project.

To Cathy: You sacrificed so much for this book. Most of all, you gave up time with me. You shared me with books, articles, podcasts, glowing computer screens, three writing retreats away from you, and countless hours on weekends. I am the most fortunate man alive for doing life with you.

To Christy, Rebecca, and Heidi: You are the greatest adult children anyone could possibly have. You fill me with such joy. Okay, a few times of angst, but now I have this book to help me.

To Randy Bramel, Rod Emery, Terry Hartshorn, Tom Purcell, and Steve Bowie: I am deeply grateful for our time together on Tuesday mornings. What a group of amazing men to do life with, along with some fun fishing trips.

To Todd Dean: Your friendship and leadership as board chair at HomeWord have not only guided this ministry but deeply shaped my life. I'm grateful for your wisdom and heart.

To Andrea Palpant: I am honored that you are my editor on this project. You made this a much better book. Thank you so much for pouring your insight and talent into every page.

To my fellow *New Life LIVE* radio hosts: It's a joy to share the mic with you. What an honor to sit with such gifted and compassionate counselors.

To the HomeWord team: What a pleasure to work together to "help families succeed." From our podcasts to conferences to social media and all the rest, it is so good to work alongside such wonderful and gifted men and women.

To Greg Johnson: There has never been a better literary agent. You took a chance on me many years ago, and I've never forgotten it. Thank you for believing in the message and the messenger.

QUESTIONS FOR REFLECTION AND DISCUSSION

Chapter 1: From Heartache to Hope

1. Both heartache and hope are powerful emotions. On a scale from 1 to 5 (5 being the most intense), how would you rate the level of heartache and hope you feel today in relation to your adult child (or children)?
2. The Eric story is a tremendous story of hope as he walked back into church and sat by his mom. His parents "stayed in the story." What advice would you give to someone who is considering stepping out of their adult child's story?
3. Do you have a "circle of support"? Who are some of your circle of support people? If you don't have much of a circle of support, where can you find that kind of support?

4. What can you do to "create a welcome mat culture" for your adult child?
5. It can be very easy to give in to fear and heartache instead of focusing on hope. What specifically can you do to bring hope to the forefront of your mind and heart, even when it's hard?

Chapter 2: Be the Adult in the Room

1. What makes it especially challenging to be consistent about "being the adult in the room" with your adult child?
2. Embracing the shift from being in a strong authority position with your adult child to a role of guidance, support, and offering wisdom usually isn't easy. How do you handle the situation when you offer good advice and your adult child doesn't follow it?
3. To lead with love and kindness takes discipline on your part. How do you navigate the challenge of showing loving acceptance of your adult child without it being mistaken for unconditional approval?
4. Do you want to be right or to improve your relationship? Sometimes you can't have it both ways. Do you agree with this principle? If you do agree, how can you best handle a complicated situation with your adult child while applying this principle?
5. Think about the term *living martyr.* What do you think that concept means? Do you awfulize or know

someone who does? How can this be detrimental to personal growth for both parent and child?

Chapter 3: You Are Not Defined by Your Adult Child's Choices

1. Some parents think they are defined by their children's poor choices. They blame themselves. Do you find yourself caught in this mindset? Why or why not?
2. Overthinking can be about more than our adult children; it can be a pattern for how we look at life. Would you define yourself as an overthinker? Why or why not?
3. "Reframe your mindset" is a key principle in this book. Try one "reframe your mindset" exercise right now. Identify a troubling fact from your life. Now ask yourself, "What else is true?" How can this reframing exercise be beneficial to you?
4. Counselor Kathy Cunningham uses the phrase "acceptance without approval." How does this concept apply to your relationship with your adult child?
5. The account of Dr. Sam and his patient at the end of the chapter is a story of hope. The former drug addict said to him ten years later, "Thank you for believing in me." How could this be played out in your relationship with your adult child?

Chapter 4: Learn to Live Above Your Circumstances

1. "Your circumstance may not change, but your attitude can change, and that makes all the difference in the world." What makes this concept both a powerful tool toward more connection with your adult child and a challenge to carry throughout your life?
2. This chapter and much of the book focuses on parents becoming the very best version of themselves in order to prepare for potential storms. Where have you done this well, and where do you sense you've built on sand instead?
3. "Before freedom comes pain." How can this principle work in your own life?
4. Healing doesn't happen in isolation. Do you have replenishing relationships in your life? If not, where will you find them, and who could they possibly be in your life?
5. "Maturing is realizing how many things do not require your comment" (Rachel Wolchin). How can practicing this concept strengthen your deeper connection with your adult child?

Chapter 5: Setting Boundaries and Fostering a Good Relationship with Your Adult Child

1. When have you ever had a time similar to Tom and Kelsey's when clear boundaries and expectations were not expressed and it brought tension to your relationship with your adult child?

2. How well have you established healthy boundaries and expectations? What steps can you take to improve communication with your adult child?
3. What makes it difficult to respect the boundaries your adult child sets?
4. Do you see any codependent patterns in your life? If so, what changes could move you toward greater emotional health? (Taking the Codependent Relationship Quiz on page 81 might be a healthy exercise for you.)
5. How can setting up clear boundaries with your adult child help contribute to stronger self-control and self-care for your own life and your adult child's?

Chapter 6: The Deconstruction of Your Adult Child's Faith and What to Do About It

1. Can you relate to this idea of deconstruction of your adult child's faith? If so, how does it make you feel?
2. The anatomy of an atrophied faith (neglect, drift, unbelief or lack of trust, disobedience, insensitivity to God, forfeiting spiritual purpose) is an important concept in this chapter. Do you relate to these stages? What thoughts might you add to this idea that people "drift away"?
3. David Kinnaman describes these wandering adults as nomads, prodigals, and exiles. Does your adult child fit into any of these categories? From reading this chapter, what is one new insight you learned about supporting your adult child?

4. Which of the five action steps for responding to deconstruction was most helpful to you (pages 99–103)?
5. What can you do today to feel more hopeful about your adult child's spiritual journey of faith?

Chapter 7: Estrangement from Your Adult Child and How to Heal

1. There may not be a more heartbreaking situation in life than estrangement from a child. Parents often need to take the lead in reconciliation, even when it means holding back their desire to criticize. How do you feel about that advice?
2. Common consequences of estrangement are shame, anger, guilt, resentment, desperation, and grief. What other consequences of estrangement have you experienced or observed in a relationship?
3. *Complicated bereavement* is a very descriptive phrase. Have you ever experienced it, and how did you work through it?
4. The words "I'm sorry" are a powerful diffuser of intense feelings. Have you witnessed or experienced a heartfelt apology in your life that made a difference? Why is it difficult to apologize when you feel more right than wrong in a relationship?
5. The idea of embracing a relationship even when you have quite different views on life and lifestyle is a tough concept but key to moving forward. What is

one thing you can do to make that more of a reality in the relationship with your adult child?

Chapter 8: When Your Relationship Is Toxic and Complicated

1. Do any of the signs of a toxic family environment feel familiar to your experience? If so, which ones?
2. In many toxic relationships with adult children there is a long history of dysfunction in the family. If you come from that kind of background, what can you do to be a transitional generation that moves toward greater emotional health for the family?
3. This chapter closes with an illustration from the movie *We Bought a Zoo*. The dad in the story said, "All you need is twenty seconds of insane courage. . . . And I promise you, something great will come of it." Are you facing any decisions right now that require twenty seconds of "insane courage"?
4. What would you say is something that could help heal toxicity in your family?
5. How has seeking help, support, and wisdom helped you in the past? What is one step you could take after reading this chapter that would be beneficial for you and your family?

Chapter 9: Breaking Down Walls and Building Bridges

1. "Communication is a learned trait." How does this statement strike you? Is there anything you learned

from this chapter about communication that applies to your own life?

2. We all build walls for protection. Which of the walls described in this chapter resonates most to you?
3. "With my God I can scale a wall" (Ps. 18:29). How could David's statement from so long ago speak into your present-day parenting journey today?
4. "Words don't always lead to connection. Connection leads to words." How can that concept influence your relationship with your adult child?
5. In this chapter we learned that many young adults are moving back toward faith. How does this encourage you? How can this Scripture verse be helpful to you? "Devote yourselves to prayer, being watchful and thankful" (Col. 4:2).

From the Publisher

ARE EVEN BETTER WHEN THEY'RE SHARED!

Help other readers find this one:

- Post a review at your favorite online bookseller
- Post a picture on a social media account and share why you enjoyed it
- Send a note to a friend who would also love it—or better yet, give them a copy

Thanks for reading!

www.ingramcontent.com/pod-product-compliance
Lightning Source LLC
LaVergne TN
LVHW030920080826
845145LV00013B/2988

* 9 7 8 0 3 1 0 3 7 0 4 7 5 *